Akashic Records

Accessing Past Lives and Universal Knowledge through Connecting with Spirit Guides, Meditation, Prayer, Chakra Balancing, and Raising Your Vibration

© Copyright 2022 - All rights reserved.

The content contained within this book may not be reproduced, duplicated, or transmitted without direct written permission from the author or the publisher.

Under no circumstances will any blame or legal responsibility be held against the publisher, or author, for any damages, reparation, or monetary loss due to the information contained within this book, either directly or indirectly.

Legal Notice:

This book is copyright protected. It is only for personal use. You cannot amend, distribute, sell, use, quote, or paraphrase any part, or the content within this book, without the consent of the author or publisher.

Disclaimer Notice:

Please note the information contained within this document is for educational and entertainment purposes only. All effort has been executed to present accurate, up-to-date, reliable, complete information. No warranties of any kind are declared or implied. Readers acknowledge that the author is not engaging in the rendering of legal, financial, medical, or professional advice. The content within this book has been derived from various sources. Please consult a licensed professional before attempting any techniques outlined in this book.

By reading this document, the reader agrees that under no circumstances is the author responsible for any losses, direct or indirect, that are incurred as a result of the use of the information contained within this document, including, but not limited to, errors, omissions, or inaccuracies.

Free limited time bonus

Stop for a moment. I have a free bonus set up for you. The problem is that we forget 90% of everything that we read after 7 days. Crazy fact, right? Here's the solution: we've created a printable, 1-page pdf summary for this book that you're reading now. All you have to do to get your free pdf summary is to go to the following website: **https://livetolearn.lpages.co/silviahill/**
Once you do, it will be intuitive. Enjoy, and thank you!

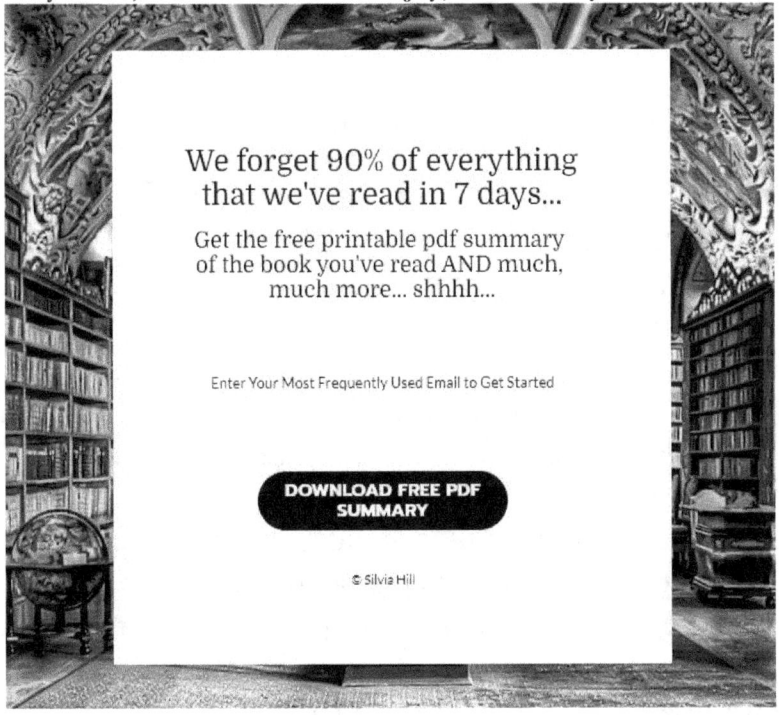

Contents

INTRODUCTION 1
CHAPTER 1: OUR WORLD AND THE AKASHA 3
    Understanding Akasha 3
    Akasha in Theosophy 9
    The Theosophist Planes of Existence 10
    Akasha and Magic 12
    The Akashic Records 13
CHAPTER 2: WHAT ARE THE AKASHIC RECORDS? 16
    Benefits of Unlocking the Akashic Records 17
    What Can You Expect from the Akashic Records? 21
    Things to Consider before Accessing the Akashic Records 22
CHAPTER 3: KARMA AND THE KARMIC CYCLE 27
    What Is Karma? 27
    The Understanding of Karma in Hinduism 29
    Karma and Karmic Cycle in Buddhism 30
    Different Types of Karmic Cycles 31
    Signs That You're Receiving a Karmic Lesson 33
    How to Break a Karmic Cycle 34
    How to Integrate a Karmic Lesson 37
    Akashic Records and How They Connect with Past Lives 38
CHAPTER 4: RAISING YOUR VIBRATION 40

WHAT IS VIBRATIONAL ENERGY? ... 43
THE MIND AND VIBRATION ... 44
VIBRATIONAL ENERGY AND THE BODY ... 45
HOW TO IMPROVE VIBRATIONAL ENERGY ... 46

CHAPTER 5: CHAKRAS 101 ... 54
WHY ARE THE CHAKRAS IMPORTANT? ... 54
THE HISTORY OF CHAKRAS ... 55
FLOW OF ENERGY ... 55
ALIGNING THE CHAKRAS TO ACCESS THE AKASHIC RECORDS ... 61
FIND OUT WHICH OF YOUR CHAKRAS NEEDS BALANCING ... 62

CHAPTER 6: UNBLOCKING THE CHAKRAS ... 69
THE IMPORTANCE OF THE CHAKRAS ... 70
UNBLOCKING THE SEVEN MAJOR CHAKRAS ... 71

CHAPTER 7: CLEANSING YOUR MIND ... 82
SPIRITUAL MEDITATION ... 84
REIKI ... 85
PAST LIFE REGRESSION MEDITATION ... 89
SYMPTOMS OF AN UNCLEAR MIND ... 90

CHAPTER 8: CLEANSING YOUR SPACE ... 94
SMUDGING ... 95
INCENSE CLEANSING ... 97
SOUND CLEANSING ... 100

CHAPTER 9: CONNECTING TO YOUR SPIRIT GUIDES ... 103
HOW TO CONNECT WITH YOUR SPIRIT GUIDE ... 105
TYPES OF SPIRIT GUIDES ... 109

CHAPTER 10: IDENTIFY YOUR INTENTIONS ... 112
THE IMPORTANCE OF INTENTION ... 114
SETTING YOUR INTENTIONS ... 116

CHAPTER 11: THE PRAYER METHOD ... 119
THE BENEFITS OF THE PRAYER METHOD ... 120
PRAYERS FOR OPENING AND CLOSING THE AKASHIC RECORDS ... 122
ADDITIONAL TIPS FOR USING THE PRAYER METHOD ... 126

CHAPTER 12: THE MEDITATION METHOD ... 128
MEDITATION ... 128

How to Meditate to Access Akashic Records 129
CHAPTER 13: THE VISUALIZATION METHOD 135
What Is Visualization? 135
Akashic Records Are the Library of the Soul 136
Visualization and Akashic Records 136
How to Practice Visualization 137
Frequency of Practice 138
Simple Visualization Techniques for Beginners 139
Accessing Akashic Records via Visualization 143
Beginner Guidance for Accessing Akashic Records 145
CHAPTER 14: ACCESSING OTHERS' RECORDS 146
The Challenges of Accessing Others' Records 147
The Process of Accessing Others' Records 147
It Starts with You 149
Practice Is Important 150
Additional Tips for Accessing Others' Records 151
CHAPTER 15: AKASHIC RECORDS FAQS 155
CHAPTER 16: REACHING THE AKASHIC RECORDS IN 30 DAYS 166
30-Day Guide to Reaching Akashic Records 168
Dos and Don'ts 174
Tips and Guidelines 176
CONCLUSION 181
HERE'S ANOTHER BOOK BY SILVIA HILL THAT YOU MIGHT LIKE 183
FREE LIMITED TIME BONUS 184
REFERENCES 185

Introduction

Have you ever wondered what your past lives were like? Are you curious about your future?

The Akashic Records are where all of our past, present, and future lives are stored. They're also the source of universal knowledge to help us better understand ourselves and others.

Have you ever wondered what your life would be like if you had made a different choice? What if you had taken that job offer in New York instead of staying in Chicago? What if you hadn't gone to the bar with your friends and met your spouse? You can find out all these answers by accessing the Akashic Records.

You don't have to wonder about your past lives any longer. This book will teach you how to connect with spirit guides who will reveal everything about yourself in the Akashic Records. We'll also show you how to raise your vibration to access these records more easily.

The first step in accessing the records is understanding our world as it exists today. We explore what makes up our reality, why we're here, and what happens after death. You may be surprised at some of the answers. Then we'll take a look at the Akashic Records - their purpose, history, location, and even how they work - so you will have a firm foundation for everything else that comes next.

When you read the Akashic Records, you will connect with your spirit guides, who will help guide you through this process and answer any questions that may arise during your reading. You will feel more connected than ever before and start living an inspired life full of love and light. This is truly a once-in-a-lifetime opportunity, so don't miss out.

You can learn about yourself in previous incarnations or even improve your current life. It is also an excellent way to discover why certain things happen in your life and learn from mistakes made in the past.

We also give step-by-step instructions on how to unblock your chakras (energy centers), work together more effectively, and cleanse yourself and the space around you before reading the records together. Also included are tips on how best to connect with spirit guides (helpers from the spiritual realm), an essential part of accessing universal knowledge through connecting with spirit guides during readings.

If anything is holding us back from reaching our full potential, it's fear. Fear of failure or success, fear of change or lack thereof, but whatever it may be for each individual, it will always hold some power over us until we face it head-on and overcome it. This book teaches readers how to connect with these spirit guides to gain insight and to overcome their fears once and for all.

"Akashic Records" is a practical guide that teaches you how to access the records of your past, present, and future life to understand yourself and those around you better. If you are looking for guidance on overcoming fear, this book is for you.

Chapter 1: Our World and the Akasha

If you've ever tried to understand your true purpose in life, you've probably encountered the term Akashic Records. As one of the core concepts of theosophy, these records are essentially a collection of everything that has ever happened in the world and will ever happen in the future. They don't only include a record of the actual events that have and will occur; they also include the thoughts, feelings, and intent of every human who ever lived and will ever live.

When used correctly, these records can help you reach a higher level of understanding. However, before you can understand how to access the Akashic Records, you'll first need to understand precisely what they are.

Understanding Akasha

Before we get to the Akashic Records themselves, readers should first attempt to understand the concept of Akasha. This concept is utilized to explain the Akashic Records.

First, let's understand what "Akasha" means.

"Akasha" is a Sanskrit word. Depending on how it is translated, it can mean any of the following things:

- Ether
- Sky
- Atmosphere
- Open space
- To be visible

In everyday speech, a version of the word ("akash") describes the sky. However, the word has a much deeper meaning in Hinduism and other traditional Indian religions (like Jainism and Buddhism).

Understanding Indian Cosmology

There are several models of Indian cosmology. However, the *pancha mahabhuta* system is most common and talks about five or six major cosmological elements. These elements are:

- Earth, or *prithvi*
- Water, or *jal/varuna (apa* in some traditions)
- Fire, or *agni (teja* in some traditions)
- Air and wind, or *vayu*
- Space, or *Akasha/dyaus*

In Buddhism, the elements are a little more complex than described above. For example, Akasha is split into two halves: *Akasha-dhatu*, which translates to limited space, and *ajatakasa*, meaning endless space.

So, what does this all mean?

Again, each element mentioned above has a different meaning in Indian cosmology. These are:

- **Earth:** The element that all other elements build on. It represents solidity, the physicality of humans, and forms the basis of our lives. The element is part of the physical matter around us and a part of our minds.

- **Water:** The element that represents perpetual motion and fluidity. Simultaneously, there is a quality of memory within the element of water – scientific evidence shows that water has memory, and how you approach the water will affect how it shapes itself.

- **Air:** This element doesn't just contain the oxygen and carbon dioxide you breathe in and out. Rather, it references all atmospheric elements, including those still being discovered. Like the breath you exhale, the element of air is one of the most "repulsive," just like air is forcefully repulsed and removed from your body.

- **Fire:** In Hinduism, the element of fire is represented by a two-faced deity, symbolic of fire that both gives and takes life. This element literally represents fire, but it also represents heat and energy in general – any processes involving heat and energy production can be related to fire, including internal bodily processes.

- **Ether/Space:** The element of Akasha is not empty space – it is one of the subtlest elements of existence and is the space where everything exists. It is an imperceptible force, and the rest of the world comes from Akasha. As for the human body, the Akashic element comprises the body's orifices, such as the ears and mouth.

In Buddhist traditional cosmology and throughout greater parts of the Indian subcontinent, these five elements are described as being within the person or located outside the person. For example, outside the body could be in a river or a mountain.

Additionally, there is a sixth element involved in cosmology in some traditions, which is the consciousness, or *vinnana*. This element refers to the three "basic" feelings of the human condition – pleasure, pain, and the sensation of neither pleasure nor pain. It also covers the sense impressions that cause these emotions within the individual.

In some scientific analyses of the five elements, the first four – earth, water, air, and fire – are

considered aspects of every object in the world. So:

- **Earth** represents the density of the object.

- **Water** represents fluidity, viscosity, and solubility.

- **Air** represents the pressure of an object and the reactant force that acts on objects.

- **Fire** represents heat energy. Although some texts refer to two types of fire elements – the heat of the fire and the heat of coldness – modern science shows that the sensation of feeling cold is merely a result of having less heat energy around you, meaning that both types of fire element ultimately relate back to heat energy.

However, Akasha is a little less understandable by modern science. Let's look at what this element represents in traditional Indian religion:

- **Buddhism:** As mentioned above, in Buddhism, the idea of the Akasha element is divided into two halves which consist of limited space referred to as Akasha-dhatu, and endless space or *ajatakasa*. Buddhism explicitly says that the Akasha element is real, and understanding it is often identified as the fifth state of dhyana or meditation.

- **Jainism:** As with other religions and traditions, Akasha is identified as space in Jainism. It is one of the six essential substances of creation and helps facilitate the other five (sentient beings or souls, non-sentient matter, and the principles of motion, rest, and time). Without Akasha, the other five could not exist. Akasha is infinite and all-pervading and comprises infinite space points. In some Jain traditions, and like Buddhism, there are two types of Akasha – loakasha, the space occupied by the material world, and aloakasha, the space beyond the material world, which is empty and essentially an absolute void. As we understand it, the universe is only a small part of the loAkasha. At the highest point of loAkasha is the siddhashila (essentially, the home of souls liberated from the cycle of birth and death and achieved moksha).

Akasha is also important in **Hinduism**.

In Vedic Hinduism, Akasha is the first of the five elements to be created. The sequence for the creation of the elements is recorded in a Vedic mantra, which explains:

- First, space (Akasha) appeared
- From space came air
- From air came fire (or energy)

- From fire came water
- Finally, water gave birth to the earth

The main characteristic of Akasha is shabda, or sound. In Hinduism, shabda and artha are eternal, and the sound defined by *shabda* represents gaining necessary or proper knowledge. So, in Hinduism, Akasha is linked to knowledge.

Some Hindu texts explain that Akasha is the same as ether, and it is not only an element but the fifth **physical** element. Therefore, they hold it to be real and corporeal.

However, other traditions explain that sound is the only property of Akasha. Others translate the word Akasha to mean firmament – meaning the heavens – and explain that it is also one of the names of Shiva, one of the primary Hindu deities and the God of Destruction, Yoga, Time, and Dance. He is a member of the Trimurti of Brahma, Vishnu, and Shiva, and with them, he helps guide the world through the cycles of creation and destruction.

In most Indian traditions, Akasha is the most important element. Without Akasha, the other elements – the four other elements described in Buddhism and Hinduism, or the five other essential substances described in Jainism – would not exist.

Akasha may not always be considered a physical element, but it is still more important than the physical elements. While the sixth non-physical element (vinnana or consciousness) is often not mentioned in the exploration of the essential elements in Indian cosmology, Akasha remains a crucial part of understanding the universe around us.

In yogic traditions, all five elements mentioned above need to collaborate. If they are not in harmony, it becomes a struggle to achieve your goals. In Isha yoga, every part of your yogic practice is based on getting these five elements in harmony, allowing you to reap the benefits of each element and also the combination of them all. This yoga tradition believes that getting the five elements in harmony makes life significantly easier for the individual.

Akasha in Theosophy

Theosophy is a religious movement that teaches the values of social improvement and universal brotherhood and explains that there is a single, divine Absolute. Everything in the universe is an outward reflection from the Absolute, and theosophy promotes the idea that the purpose of life is to attain spiritual emancipation.

Many of the basic principles of theosophy are derived from the writings of Russian Helena Blavatsky, and she is often considered the founder of theosophy. One of the key parts of theosophy, at least according to Blavatsky's writings, was the idea of Akasha.

In her writings, Blavatsky referred to Akasha as essentially being a life force. She also spoke about the "tablets of the astral light," which document the past and the future and contain all human thought and action on them.

Other explorations of the term Akasha by Blavatsky include explaining that it is a name for the "eternal divine consciousness." It is infinite, unconditioned, and undifferentiated.

In theosophy, logos is the "manifested deity" and the "outward expression" of the Absolute. Blavatsky explains that there are three logoi. The first is unmanifested, the pre-cosmic ideation that first emanates from the Absolute. There is no time or space at this stage, and these are only formed once differentiation sets in. The first logos is essentially symbolic of unrecognized potential, which nonetheless still exists.

Per Blavatsky, this first logos radiates from Akasha. Without Akasha, the first logos of pure potential is impossible, and so is the world as we know it.

Essentially, Blavatsky's writings use Akasha as another way to refer to the divine Absolute of theosophy. Akasha radiates everything else, and without Akasha, there is no universe - just as with the Absolute.

Blavatsky never used the term "Akashic Records" in her writings. However, as mentioned above, she talked about tablets in which all human thoughts and actions were recorded. The idea of the Akashic Records was explored in detail by two prominent theosophists - Alfred Percy Sinnett and Henry Steel Olcott.

Olcott explains (as discussed above) that there are two enteral ideas in Buddhism - nirvana and Akasha. Everything comes from the Akashic element, and nothing emerges from nothing. He notes that this essentially meant that there was "a permanency of the records in the Akasha" in early Buddhism. People could also read these records, which were granted when a person reached enlightenment.

The Theosophist Planes of Existence

In theosophy, there are six (or seven) planes of existence. While Blavatsky described seven planes, the first is occasionally omitted in modern theosophic writings.

These planes are essentially formed in circles. The first is the smallest, at the center, and the seventh encompasses the other six and is the largest. The seven planes, from the inside out, are:

1. Sthula Sharira, or the Prakritic plane, encompasses the physical body.

2. Linga Sharira, or the Astral plane, is the plane of the astral body.

3. The Pranic, or Jivic plane, is the residence of the vital principal.

4. The Kamarupa, or Fohatic plane, is the location of the "desired body" - the base of passions and desires.

5. The Manasic, or Mahatic plane, is the seat of the higher ego (the spiritual aspect) and the lower ego (the aspect of the ego covered by the ordinary mind). This is the plane where the Akasha is said to reside.

6. The Buddhic, or Alayic plane, is the home of the universal spirit. It is from this plane that divine inspiration emanates.

7. The Atmic, or Auric plane, is the plane of the Absolute, where its Radiation emanates from. For an individual to reach this plane is to become at one with the Absolute. It is sometimes omitted, as it is the highest plane.

As mentioned above, the Akasha resides on the 5th plane. According to Blavatsky, each plane was essentially the sum of what came before it. So, the Mahatic plane was everything contained within that plane, and everything contained with the Fohatic, Jivic, Astral, and Prakritic planes.

The smaller planes would not exist without the bigger ones. Theosophist, Annie Besant, looked at the planes in terms of modern science. According to her ideas:

1. The Prakritic plane was the plane of the solid element.
2. The Astral plane was the plane of the liquid.
3. The Jivic plane was the plane of the gaseous.
4. The Fohatic plane was the plane of the etheric.
5. The Mahatic plane was the plane of the super-etheric.
6. The Buddhic plane was the plane of the subatomic.
7. The Auric plane was the plane of the atomic.

The seven planes can be divided into the heavy physical (the solid, liquid, and gaseous) and the etheric (the four higher planes – etheric, super-etheric, subatomic, and atomic).

Vital life force is found at the higher planes, so understanding these higher places is crucial.

Though Akasha is found on the 5th plane, it is also manifested on the 1st, Prakritic plane. As discussed, each of the higher planes encompasses what is contained within the smaller planes.

However, the Prakritic plane is the plane of matter – the manifestations of Absolute's Radiation. The Akasha is the higher aspect of this manifestation, and all matter from the Akasha.

Moreover, it should be noted that even though Akasha is on the fifth plane, it is still infinite, and this is why some theorists refer to the Seven Planes as the Seven Principles of Akasha. Therefore, although the Akasha resides in the 5th plane, it is still undeniably connected to the 7th plane and the divine Absolute.

Akasha and Magic

Aside from being the source of esoteric knowledge, Akasha is also connected with magic. According to Blavatsky, Akasha is linked to the power allowing magic to function. She wrote that "The Akasha is the indispensable agent of every kritya (magical performance) religious or profane."

Keep in mind that Akasha is an essential element of creation. While it may differ in its nature and characteristics, it is a part of everything, just like the less subtle elements (fire, water, earth, etc.). To perform magic, practitioners must first understand Akasha properly because not only is it linked to the power allowing magic to function, but it is also a basic element of creation. Performing magic without a proper understanding of Akasha would be like driving a car with eyes closed while solely depending on your hearing for guidance. Not to mention, Akasha is the source of knowledge, and, in a way, it permeates all forms of life. How can one even begin to understand the workings of magic without rooting themselves in Akasha?

The Akashic Records

As already stated, Blavatsky never mentioned the word "Akashic" in her writings. However, later theorists have used her work to explore the concept of these records.

Since the Akasha is the source of knowledge and is linked to the Absolute (where all of the manifested reality radiates), it makes sense that there is a record of these radiations. However, these records are not easy to access. Their location in the higher, more spiritual planes of existence mean that it will take time and effort for an individual to access the Akashic Records.

The information held in these records can be challenging for the unprepared. For example, since the records hold all past and future information, readers could access their past and future lives.

If you're looking to access your Akashic Records, it is essential to understand the preparatory steps you must take and the necessary steps to prepare yourself to access them mentally. It is not a short process, i.e., you cannot expect to read your records within one day.

However, it can be extremely rewarding if you put in the effort.

Considering these challenges, you may wonder why reading these records is important. The next chapter will give you a deeper understanding of the Akashic Records and why you should gain access to them. Furthermore, the book also explains the karmic cycle and its relationship to the Akashic Records.

Ultimately, you will learn how to prepare yourself to access your records. This preparation involves raising your vibration, unblocking your chakras, and cleansing your mind. Remember, accessing higher planes requires you to be clear about your intentions, which is what the preparatory stage allows you to do. You will also learn to cleanse your space, connect with your spirit guides and helpers, and identify what you hope to achieve precisely from accessing your records.

Accessing your Akashic Records is best done with a clear intention in mind and questions you want your records to answer. Understanding how to focus your mind on only these key intentions makes accessing the records much easier.

Finally, you will also understand how to read the Akashic Records. There are various methods to access the records, and each method differs from person to person.

We speak about accessing your Akashic Records. However, it is possible to access other people's records. Accessing other people's records is significantly more challenging than accessing your own, but we've included an overview of accessing someone else's records if you need to.

The Akashic Records are merely a natural extension of the Akasha, which is space itself and the primordial essence that makes up all space. This fifth cosmic element may not be perceivable by most humans, but it plays a role in our everyday lives. According to Madame Blavatsky's and Alfred Percy Sinnett's writings, the earth is affected by the Akasha, particularly the Akashic magnetism, which helps restore the atmosphere's disturbed equilibrium. Accessing this element allows people to gain access to higher planes of existence and access the store of all the knowledge in the Akashic Records.

Now that you have understood what the Akasha is, you need to understand the Akashic Records in further detail before you learn how to access them. To do that, keep reading.

Chapter 2: What Are the Akashic Records?

In Akasha, every person's thoughts, emotions, and actions are stored in a higher dimension that transcends ours. This colossal compendium is known as the Akashic Records. It's essentially a database of our past, future, and present coexisting together. Moreover, it's a collection of all the knowledge and wisdom mankind has collected throughout history. Due to this, these records are not viewed as historical facts but as a guidance tool towards clearing our feelings and thoughts and are used to show us the right path.

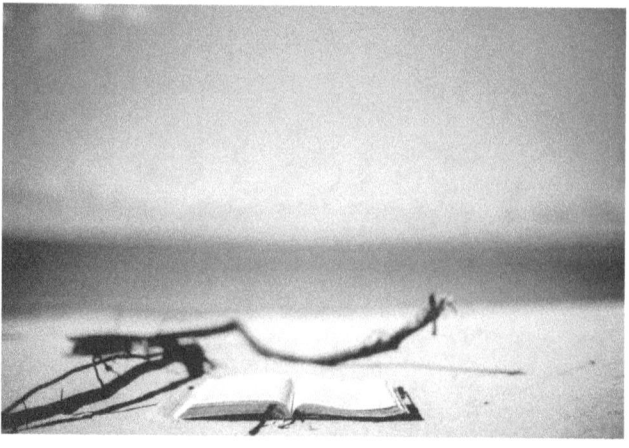

While the Akashic Records are on a higher plane, with enough practice, anyone can access theirs because, in this dimension, the natural rules, such as time, don't apply, meaning something that happened thousands of years ago is only as far away as that which happened yesterday. Akasha is the energy present in everything in the Universe - living and nonliving. Therefore, the sources of this universal wisdom are limitless. Anyone can access any record they want, from their homes or pets to their souls and relationships. Accessing Akashic Records comes with multiple benefits. Through them, you can get objective information about anything without the risk of running into judgmental opinions, like you would in any other database. In this database, there are no labels. There are only pure facts.

Benefits of Unlocking the Akashic Records

One of the largest benefits of Akashic Records is that they allow you to reflect on your choices to determine if they align with your true desires. Going through your past actions, you can know how your decisions have impacted your life so far. Let's say that you are a creative person, but to secure financial stability, you decided to take a job that requires no imagination. By going through your records, you will clearly see that your decision made you unhappy as it wasn't made with a purpose that aligns with your soul's desire. While switching to a creative career choice could make you earn less money, it would provide you with a more blissful existence.

Beyond helping you heal your internal scars, the Akashic Records can contribute to mending your relationships with your loved ones. Misunderstandings often cause most issues in relationships. If you only see things from your point of view, it clouds your judgment, which can put a strain on your relationship. The Akashic Records will help you see what is occurring between you and your loved ones from a different perspective.

Let's say a person close to you said or did something that hurt you so deeply you didn't care to hear the reasons behind their actions. By pointing out something you have missed in your interaction with them, the Records will help you move past the pain. The universal wisdom may show you that your loved one only wanted to help you by offering a neutral point of view. Once you have processed this, you can contact your loved one to mend your relationship. It will relieve the strain on your relationship and heal it over time.

Repairing broken relationships with the living is challenging enough, but the matter becomes even more complicated with the deceased. You can't make them accountable for their actions nor ask them questions about their thoughts and emotions. By accessing the Akashic Records, you gain better insight into their lives that help you understand their behavior when they were alive. It works as though you were creating a dialogue with them, except you won't speak to them; you communicate with their soul. Understanding them better helps restore your faith in your relationship and releases a burden from your soul and theirs.

Psychological trauma can sometimes transcend generations. A wrong decision your ancestors made or any ordeal they may have suffered in their lifetime can haunt you without you even realizing it.

For example, suppose your ancestor's soul has experienced trauma in childhood. In that case, they could have carried this into adulthood, preventing them from achieving their life purpose, which would have caused resentment and low expectations for the future. Furthermore, they could have also passed down this sentiment to their children, who continued on the same path with their children, and, finally, this emotional baggage ended up on their shoulders. If you experience emotional imbalance, and you can't find the cause of it in your Akashic Records, unlocking the records of your ancestors may hold the answers. Locating a past hurt and releasing it in the name of the ancestors may free your soul, too, so you can validate its desires.

Through this process, you can also discover your inner strength, which will further entice you to resolve all the dysfunctional aspects of your life. Your soul is an unchanging core of your true self and has a universal purpose of guiding you in the right directions. Through the Akashic Records, you can discover things in-depth and find out what caused you to start relying on external validation instead of listening to your own desires. An emotional trauma resulting in a fear that blocks your energy from carrying the messages from your soul may be responsible for all your actions. If it is, its traces will be present in your Akashic Records. Identifying this pattern may help you understand why you make the wrong choices in your life. Once you become aware of your action's causes and consequences, you can start making more suitable choices.

Receiving knowledge that forms part of the collective wisdom of mankind is very inspiring. The emotions the given answers evoke are often a huge source of motivation for changing one's life. It is particularly true if you are reading your Akashic Records or that of your ancestors. Generally, the closer the information is to you, the more intensely the message will be. Due to this, it will inspire you further to take the path leading you toward making your dreams come true and reaching your highest spiritual potential. If you need further motivation to surpass a particularly challenging obstacle in your life, you can tap into a special cluster of information in the Akashic Records. These are called The Grace Points, and their purpose is to help you heal the trauma caused by past events and find out what's likely to cause your inability to face the obstacle. The Grace Points also allow you to retain much more of the information you receive from the Records.

Addictions come in many forms - from physical to emotional. Sometimes they will result in you constantly ending up in toxic relationships without even being aware of this pattern. The only way to resolve this and ensure it never happens to you again is to uncover why you are attracting toxic people to your life in the first place. The reason behind this is often too painful to bear, so your mind will automatically block the memory from your conscious mind. However, the trigger remains in your subconscious, and it keeps affecting your relationships. The Akashic Records can help you find this trigger, deal with it, and erase it from your mind.

Besides being a healing medium, The Akashic Records can support your learning new skills. Part of this stems from a huge chunk of information you access from your loved ones - the living and the dead. By lending you strength and guidance when you need it the most, even your long-passed ancestors can help you feel loved. In addition, seeking information through the records opens up a vast array of knowledge. Wanting to learn more about the various aspects of life is part of your basic human makeup. Now, you will have an infinite source of information at your disposal to satisfy your curiosity. As you learn more and start developing theories of your own, you will create new belief systems, bringing new emotions to the surface, making you invest even more into the knowledge you have gained from the Records. As the information grows more relevant to your life, it will become an integral part of your soul. In short, you become emotionally invested in your success. However, the information gained from the Records can serve as an inspiration for others, and the reason is that people notice when you genuinely believe in something. If they see how driven you are in your chosen path in life, this may motivate them to make the necessary changes in their lives, too, whereas if just preaching to them about making better life choices, you can show them what decisions led to your happiness, and they will more likely adopt your beliefs rather than learning from any lecture.

The Akashic Records can channel through various methods of meditation, prayer, or intuition retrieval techniques, but you can also use these to heal. By combining the Records' wisdom with a relaxation technique of your choice, you can achieve results much faster. However, these specific exercises aren't the only way to heal your past traumas. Universal wisdom can even inspire you in your hobbies, helping you become better at something you enjoy doing is another way to promote self-healing. You may even find a new permanent vocation through this and fulfill your desires in a way you never thought possible.

What Can You Expect from the Akashic Records?

The Akashic Records can provide you with answers anytime you need them. As long as your questions are focused on the subject whose Records you are accessing, you will get an answer on anything you can imagine. For example, if you are reading for yourself, ask questions pertaining to anything that has to do with your life. You can unlock the Records of your cat if you want to, but the inquiry has to be related to you. It's worth mentioning that you can only expect answers to open-ended questions because the wisdom in Akasha is kept in a universal language. To understand the message, it must be translated to your language by the Recordkeepers. These beings prefer not to convey answers to yes or no questions because they know that these questions cannot have a definite answer. Answering with a simple yes or no would deceive you, and this is something the Records will never do.

On the other hand, if you are looking for guidance or a way to empower yourself to make a life-altering decision, you can rely on the Records. The purpose of this universal source of wisdom is to promote self-reliance. You can use it to learn life lessons on your own, but you will always be able to rely on it throughout your journey. Sometimes the information you get is much less than you would have hoped for because you only receive what you need and not what you think you need. While we often carry deep traumas from the past, we also tend to make our problems bigger than they actually are. If you receive a short answer, you are lucky because your issue can be solved much quicker than you think.

Ultimately, you can expect the Akashic Records to get to the root of the issue and, more importantly, help resolve it. As soon as you open the Records, their energy will encompass you, lending you that initial boost of confidence you need to unlock the required information. Moving further, by asking many specific questions, you can revisit all the events from your life that may have caused trauma.

Things to Consider before Accessing the Akashic Records

When accessing specific Akashic Records, you must ask them precisely formulated questions. You will get a more straightforward answer and a clearer idea of how to proceed using the guidance you have received. For beginners, it's a good idea to write these questions down beforehand, so you can keep them in front of you when trying to access the Records. Otherwise, you can run into the danger of your mind being waylaid by unrelated thoughts and emotions, not to mention that even remembering the messages you received can be challenging for a beginner. You may see the information clearly when accessing it. However, as soon as you close the Records, your recollection of what transpired can become hazy. Write down the answers immediately after receiving them and while your line of communication with the Akashic Records is still open. Rereading your notes will keep the takeaways fresh after closing the Records.

Being clear about what you wish to learn from the Records has one more advantage. This medium contains a vast amount of information. Due to this, the only way to ensure you get the right answer is by stating your intention clearly. Otherwise, it would be like randomly browsing a database hoping to find interesting information. Even if you just want to explore a certain period of your life because you aren't sure when the event happened, you will still need to make this clear right from the start. Finding a more specific answer will be nearly impossible without narrowing your intention. You could spend weeks browsing through the Records and still won't find what you are looking for if you can't formulate your questions clearly enough.

It's equally important to remember that the rules of science do not apply in Akasha, meaning that going in with a scientific preconception or searching for an explanation for your answer rigidly and systematically won't get you the desired results. On the other hand, you can get empowerment from the wisdom and energy of all dimensions and use it in your lifetime with the right approach. The best way to look at the Akashic Records is as a collective spiritual consciousness evolving since the dawn of mankind. Accessing this collective wisdom requires cultivating a sacred relationship with your spirituality. Only those seekers who have reached a state of spiritual independence will access the infinite sources of energy and knowledge in Akasha.

If it's your first time reading about the Akashic Records, you may be a little skeptical about their existence. One reason may be that you don't have much experience exploring spirituality. We are often disconnected from our inner selves, and facing anything that may uncover it can be challenging. But, even if you tried to connect to your spirituality before, unlocking the Akashic Records can still make you feel like you are in uncharted territory. The amount of spiritual wisdom you will gain access to will be overwhelming.

Another challenge those attempting to unlock their Records often face is expecting to get precise answers for their questions about their future. The Akashic Records only show us potential outcomes, and what you see depends on several factors. The idea of tapping into this database of universal wisdom is undoubtedly intriguing. However, when looking into the future, seekers are advised not to take everything at face value. It can often result in disappointment upon discovering that the future you have foreseen doesn't come to fruition. Remember, there could be infinite outcomes to every thought and action. Therefore, the answer you get at a particular time is the most likely scenario based on your intentions at that moment.

Moreover, you are in control of shaping your destiny, and you can decide to step on a new path at any moment in life. So, a possible outcome will only materialize if you stay on the same path you are following when accessing the Records. If you diverge from it by taking one step in another direction, the results of your actions will also change.

However, instead of dwelling on why the outcomes may change, decide to focus on using the source of knowledge you gain from the records to conjure the outcome you desire. Remember, this source of wisdom is thousands of times more potent than your conscious mind, meaning it can have an immense bearing on your thought and the resulting actions. The Akashic Records can be a powerful tool, but it's up to you how you use them. And, no, the Records won't tell you what to do, either. They will, however, offer guidance that comes from a place of compassion and which promotes love. This will empower you to transcend limiting beliefs and transform your relationships, but it all happens very subtly. Most importantly, it will only work if you are willing to put in the necessary effort to transform your life.

While you may hear about popular ways to access the Akashic Records, in reality, there is no right or wrong way to do so. As long as the method you use keeps you focused enough to reach, unlock the Records, and receive their messages, it will work just fine. A grounded state is necessary for opening your mind to receive all the knowledge you seek. The information you encounter will be confusing, especially if you don't yet have enough practice retrieving it. Therefore, you want your mind to be settled and clear of irrelevant thoughts and emotions. Plus, if you receive particularly confusing advice or a piece of information that's hard to process, you may become unsettled after the session. Being in a calm state of mind beforehand helps deescalate the situation, and with enough practice, the process will become easier. After a while, even after a strenuous session, you will automatically start to do the same relaxation exercise you used to get into a relaxed state.

The Objective Nature of Akashic Records

As we've mentioned earlier, the Akashic Records only hold objective information. This is because when we think, feel, or engage in other activities, we leave impressions on our souls. These impressions and the resulting energy get stored in time and space.

Now, once we've started dealing with energy, this means we've started dealing with the rawest form of the concept, thought, or feeling. In other words, we've started dealing with what the thing is and not what it feels like, looks like, etc. For example, grief is a reaction that we often have when we suffer a loss. Subjectively, we all have opinions as to why we grieve. In addition, many may have feelings about the concept or feeling that is grief. Meanwhile, objectively, grief is simply a reaction to an event.

Accessing the Akashic Records will help you understand objective information. It is up to you to adapt the information to your core beliefs – or your core beliefs to the information – but one thing remains true: Akashic Records contain wisdom in its *rawest energy form.*

Chapter 3: Karma and the Karmic Cycle

Karma, the Karmic cycle, and Akashic Records are all interconnected with actions and deeds. As you know by now, the Akashic Records hold the key to past and future lives, so to understand them properly, you have to understand how the karmic cycle works based on a person's deeds. This chapter will give you a thorough insight on the concept of Karma, the understandings of the Karmic Cycle in different religions, and how a Karmic lesson works.

What Is Karma?

The concept of Karma is found mainly in the Hindu scripture, the Bhagavad Gita, and in many other religions, mainly Buddhism, Sikhism, and Jainism. The concept can be understood by common phrases like, "What you reap, you sow." or "What goes around, comes around." Simply put, Karma is the direct consequence of your actions, whether good or bad.

While many people use words like Karma to scare people for their misdeeds, the concept of Karma is not as simple. In actuality, Karma is neither punishment nor reward; it can be both simultaneously as a result of your actions. Karma doesn't only encompass actions but also your thoughts and your words.

If it's easier for you to understand Karma by relating it to a law of science (physics), bring Newton's third law or the law of *action and reaction* to mind. The law states that every action will have an equal and opposite reaction. Karma is somewhat like that. Your actions will define how life treats you in the long run.

For example, imagine mistreating a person for a long time, not caring about the consequences. After a while, you'll start to notice that the universe is treating you in the same way. The thing about Karma is, you'll know when it hits you. Most people are conscious when receiving Karma for any good or bad deed.

Many people think that maybe the concept of Karma was introduced to make people more conscious of their actions and their behaviors. Maybe it was supposed to keep people in check and make them scared of the consequences of their actions. Whatever the case, if you're someone wanting to relate your past lives, deeds, and misdeeds to your Akashic Records and who is working toward betterment, it's important that you understand where the concept of Karma originated from.

The Understanding of Karma in Hinduism

The word "Karma" originated from the Sanskrit word "Kri," meaning to act or react. The literal meaning of Karma can be roughly translated to something that is created or produced by one's physical organs. However, Karma encompasses physical actions, thoughts, or mental actions. There is a strong belief in Hinduism that thoughts have the power to impact others. For example, harmful thoughts will negatively affect who they are directed toward and the person directing them. This concept was associated with ancient mantras and their ability to affect people through thoughts. For example, when a mantra was used to curse someone, both people suffered as a result.

The karma incurred by a person through their actions can determine the path life takes them on. In Hinduism, Karma is said to be a regulating and correcting mechanism, and by regulating our actions, we can achieve greater things in life. Our actions have the power to mitigate or intensify our suffering. Therefore, Karma is meant to teach us lessons and regulate our actions. The sooner we learn from them, the sooner we'll move toward perfection, harmony, and peace.

Numerous references to Karma are found in the Hindu Scriptures, mainly Gita. While many of these references associate desire as the root cause of our suffering, others mention how to get rid of these actions. There is a whole chapter in the Bhagavad Gita that discusses the subject of Karma.

As far as the consequences of Karma are concerned, there is no definite time frame in which actions manifest reactions. In Hinduism, many believe that Karma from previous lifetimes can incorporate itself into a present or future life, and this is why one should understand how to read their Akashic Record and work towards breaking the karmic cycle.

Karma and Karmic Cycle in Buddhism

In Buddhism, the concept of Karma is referred to as Karmaphala. They believe that actions or deeds done with intention define the rebirth or the consequences for an individual. Actions or deeds done with ego are said to keep you in the karmic cycle, moving in a loop. In contrast, the Buddhist path shows you the way out.

The Buddhist concept is somewhat similar to the concept of Karma in Hinduism. Similar to how desire has been identified as the root cause of suffering in Hinduism, it is also defined as the cause of ego gratification in Buddhism.

When an individual experiences a pleasurable moment, the joy from that moment keeps on feeding their desire to experience more, resulting in a person's need for ego gratification and determining their future course of action. So, in Buddhist understanding, the more ego a person has, the more karma will be in their life.

The karmic cycle is a loop of Karma due to a person's deeds. The concept that Karma determines an individual's destiny or that past deeds, whether in this life or in the past, shape how a karmic loop works. The purpose of this cycle is to make someone realize their mistakes or give them a life lesson.

The law of karma states that every action, whether good or bad, will be recorded by the universe and be given back to you in one way or the other. Now, this doesn't necessarily mean that you'll get Karma back from the same source you're providing it to. For example, whether good or bad, your behavior with one person doesn't essentially mean that they'll behave the same way with you. The karmic cycle entails that your debts must be paid, and you have to face the karma that you've initiated through your actions.

If a person doesn't face all their karma in one lifetime, it gets transferred to the next, and this is why people sometimes feel they're in a karmic cycle from a previous lifetime. However, this doesn't mean that karmic cycles are limited to lifetimes. Many karmic patterns repeat themselves in under a year.

Different Types of Karmic Cycles

Karmic cycles usually last about 12 years, divided into subsequent sections in our lives. Although karmic cycles can be broken, these cycles have a way of conveying a message or life lesson to an individual and don't end until that message is accepted and learned. Let's look at the different karmic timelines in an individual's lifetime to understand better.

1. Childhood Cycle - 0 to 12 Years

The very first stage of karmic life and, at this point, the soul is entirely untethered and unaware of its past deeds. Children are called wet clay because they can be molded into any form depending on their situations and the people they're exposed to. The experiences and actions taken in this stage determine their future journey. Although an individual can get tethered to their past lifetimes at any stage, they are the most susceptible during this early stage because the traces of their past life are exceptionally strong.

2. Youth Cycle - 13 to 24 Years

The most critical stage in the karmic cycle is the youth cycle, where an individual pointedly enters into their life and makes conscious decisions. It is the point at which individuals start to look for reasoning and meaning in their lives while also tackling real-world problems like education and career decisions. At the end of this cycle, an individual transitions into an adult, which is when they truly start connecting with their past self. Here, people have to face many problems and debts from their previous lifetimes. For example, if an individual is usually emotionally strong, this is when they'll feel doubt overshadowing their thoughts.

3. Adult Creation - 25 to 36 Years

As soon as an individual enters adulthood, i.e., 25, their karmic patterns are formed. At this point, karma is all set due to their actions, thoughts, and behaviors. Here, the past life debt also comes into play and manifests itself in the individual's life. Any mental, emotional, and physical health challenges will manifest in your life at this point. If these karmic debts are negative, they will not be easy to get rid of, whereas any positive debts will result in better luck and successful life choices.

4. Adult Expansion - 37 to 48 Years

At this stage, the karmic patterns are at their highest intensity. Karmic life tests are extremely complex at this point, pushing a person to understand the life lessons thrown at them due to the individual's inability to understand or grasp the karmic patterns, or they're resisting karmic lessons.

So, if a person successfully grasps and understands karmic patterns before the adult expansion stage, deeper issues and Karmic patterns will emerge. Otherwise, an individual will be dealt with the same karmic pattern over and over again. The repetitive nature of these lessons and situations will only make them more agonizing for the individual.

5. Adult Contraction - 49 to 60 Years

This stage is the weakest for karmic patterns because the karmic force declines. The individual has either faced and accepted the karmic lesson or delayed it until the next lifetime. However, if an individual still feels they can settle previous debts, this is the best time to ensure they don't face problems in their next lifetime. Although the karmic patterns are weak at this point, they do not entirely vanish.

Signs That You're Receiving a Karmic Lesson

Karmic lessons are situations or patterns trying to convey a specific message to an individual. These lessons are often repetitive and don't stop emerging until we learn something from them. While every karmic lesson is unique, the most common themes emerge in relationships. These themes include your self-worth, ability to love, how you relate to yourself, and your capability to move on. To learn from a karmic lesson, you first have to identify it, so look out for the following signs in your life.

1. You're in Situations That Bring Up the Same Theme

Karmic lessons emerge in repetitive patterns that trigger an individual's same emotions and consequences. One of the most obvious signs of a karmic lesson is that you keep ending up in similar situations with the same theme and the same emotional rollercoasters. This repetitiveness, or rather stagnancy, is the universe's way of communicating that there is a lesson you must wrap your head around for you to move forward –for you to stop acting in the way that inevitably leads you to collide with a certain theme.

2. Your Relationships Have Repeated Patterns

If you feel like all your relationships, platonic or romantic, have similar patterns and red flags, it's usually a sign from the universe for a lesson to be learned. Circumstances, where repeated patterns result in similar red flags, convey a life lesson for you to acknowledge and learn from.

3. You're Constantly Facing Your Fears

Karmic lessons are said to attract relationships and circumstances that make you face your worst fears. These could be commitment issues, loneliness, expressing your feelings, etc. When faced with these challenges, you should assume a lesson to be learned.

4. You Feel Hypercritical

If you're constantly avoiding a karmic lesson, it could result in feeling hypercritical about everything surrounding you, whether it's your choices, habits, or beliefs. So, it's highly essential to integrate the life lessons that karmic cycles bring.

How to Break a Karmic Cycle

A karmic cycle is meant to convey a life lesson, understanding your past deeds and the consequences of these deeds. When you want to break a karmic cycle and get your life back on track, you need to follow a thorough spiritual process, and several approaches can achieve this. The first and foremost step is to acknowledge the lesson the universe conveys to you. Then, you need to learn from your lessons. Finally, you need to act on your learning through any of the following approaches.

5. Do Good Deeds

In an attempt to break the cycle, you should do good deeds. According to the law of compensation, or even the simple concept of karma, you need to give to get. So, if you want your life to go smoothly, without many bumps in the road, ensure that you have enough good deeds to earn good karma.

Every little thing counts because you don't know what even a single good gesture could change for someone else. Whether it's providing someone with food or donating old clothes, every good deed increases your chances of breaking a bad karmic cycle, whether from this life or previous ones.

6. Remain in Your Present Circumstances

This approach is the best way to end a bad karmic cycle and get your life right for people who don't want to follow the spiritual process. By staying in the present circumstances, doing what you can, and focusing on your present actions and deeds, you'll negate the karmic cycle that's disrupting your life.

When you are mindful of your actions and behavior, you'll see an automatic change in your behavior and observe your life getting onto the right track. To achieve this, practice effective mindfulness and be conscious of every action and every decision you take.

7. Keep Doing the Right Thing

As you're well aware, karma can be connected to previous lifetimes, and karmic cycles are pretty difficult to get out of without first understanding the concept of multiple lifetimes. When you've grasped this concept, it's important that you keep doing the right thing, good deeds, and actions over a few lifetimes. After a while, although gradually, you will undoubtedly see a difference in your life, and karmic balance will be achieved.

8. Change Your Perspective

If you're familiar with the law of attraction and how you attract what you focus on, you can understand how to break a karmic cycle by changing your perspective. When you have control over your thoughts, you'll dispel the negativity of a bad karmic cycle and attract positive experiences and people. For example, at times, when you feel like you're not good enough or you can't complete a particular task, you need to change your thoughts and stand your ground.

9. Focus On Your Choices

Choices have tremendous power to change your life, for the better or worse. Many spiritual leaders think that if you step back and reconsider your choices, your life could go a lot smoother. When making a choice, ask yourself these two questions:

- What will the consequences be after choosing this option?
- Will the choice bring positivity and happiness to me and those around me?

If you have convincing answers to these questions, and they bring you a step closer to becoming a better person, then go ahead and make that choice. If not, stop and rethink your choice once more.

10. Minimize the Bad Karma

Bad karma is a direct consequence of your bad behavior and your actions toward other people. As the rule of karma states, it doesn't matter if the people cursed you or not. Your actions have an equal reaction. So, if you want your karmic cycle to break, you must minimize bad karma. You can do this by apologizing to the people you've hurt and behaved badly toward. Also, counter your bad deeds with good ones, and promise not to repeat them.

11. Reflect

Reflection isn't an approach on its own - it is a supplementary approach to the rest. After having learned a lesson and acted upon your knowledge to change your current situation, it's crucial to look back and reflect. This will help cement the lesson, but more importantly, it will help you understand where you went wrong and why you went wrong in the first place. More often than not, you'll find that your karmic lessons share certain characteristics.

As you reflect, remember to do so gently and without judgment. We all make mistakes and learn from them. Mistakes do not speak to your *worth* - but instead to your wounds and wisdom.

How to Integrate a Karmic Lesson

You need to integrate the lessons you learned from a karmic cycle into your life to ensure that it won't repeat itself again.

1. Get in Touch with Your Values

Sometimes, we tend to fall out of tune with our values. Whether to fit in or "loosen up a little," problems mostly seem to come up when we're not living our truth. Our values are incredibly important because they allow us to grow and evolve. They are a necessary aspect when it comes to creating our desired futures.

2. You Need to Live Your Life for Yourself

We often forget that we are supposed to live life for ourselves. We tend to waste all our time trying to please others or worrying about what they think of us. However, it slips our minds that no one knows us the way we know ourselves. You're also the only person who really knows what's best for you on your life journey. So, instead of being overly concerned about others, you need to consider working on pursuing your own happiness. You also need to spend time appreciating all the good things in your life.

3. Work On Self-Compassion

Self-love and compassion are among the most, if not the most, important qualities in life. The way we treat and feel about ourselves sets the tone for all our interactions. It also affects our tendency to learn from our past mistakes. We need compassion and tolerance to be able to move past unpleasant experiences and work on becoming better versions of ourselves. This will never be possible if you feel resentful or regretful. Self-love and compassion fuel self-trust. Self-trust nourishes our faith and therefore makes us stronger. When we're strong enough, we can move on and accept our learning pace. We also don't settle for the things that we once allowed for.

4. Refine Your Intuition and Improve Your Independence

Depending on others can sway our morals and truth. You may end up leaving everything you stand for behind just to keep others in your life. Working on self-sufficiency and independence can help you stay true to yourself. You can also meditate and practice opening your third-eye chakra to refine your intuition. Our gut feelings are vital when it comes to aligning with our truth. These are all things that will help you face your karmic lessons so you can completely break the cycle and ensure that it never repeats itself.

5. Don't Doubt the Journey

Karmic cycles can be disruptive and can cause a lot of pain. However, this is the only way that you can truly let go of harmful habits and things that don't serve you in life so you can make space for better things. These lessons are not a walk in the park, which is why the only way to make it through is by trusting that these are the ones that we need to learn. Trust the process and ensure that your life is playing out exactly as it should. The earlier you break the cycle, the less pain that you'll have to endure in your lifetime.

Akashic Records and How They Connect with Past Lives

The Akashic Records can help individuals to connect with their past and present lifetimes and work through each trauma one by one. Just like past life karma affects us in the next lifetime, we also carry past life trauma into the next life. This can result in feelings of unexplainable sorrow, constantly emerging problems, and emotional baggage you can't connect with your present life.

The Akashic Records are suspended in a universal medium or energy field surrounding all of us and interpenetrate our souls. Behind the physical reality that we can see with our eyes exists a spiritual reality vibrating constantly. If you try to heal your traumas by staying in the physical realm and assuming the role of a victim, you'll never move on. Instead, you need to look past the physical realm into the spiritual universe and embrace yourself.

You need to get rid of feelings of self-doubt, victimhood, self-hatred, blaming others, and resentment completely when working with the Akashic Records. After this, you need to reach out to your inner vision and look at your problems from a different perspective.

For example, imagine you're facing a financial crisis and an urgent one at that. Now, dealing with your problems through the Akashic Records in no way means you should negate the importance of your real-life problems. Instead, what it does is help you identify the underlying causes of your problems, so you can actively work to fix them. When you look into the spiritual reality or meta-view of this financial problem, you will uncover potential reasons why you might be facing this problem. It could be a conscious or subconscious effect of your current or past life. In this case, you may have a past life trauma where money caused you trouble, so you vowed never to have too much money again.

After you've identified the cause or potential cause of your problems, go ahead and work toward breaking that karmic cycle. Ultimately, you're stronger than your problems and can solve anything that comes your way. With the help of the Akashic Records, it'll be easier to identify your dilemmas and work on them from a spiritual perspective.

Chapter 4: Raising Your Vibration

As you can tell from the discussion so far, the Akashic Records have the potential to play an important and pivotal role in our lives if we can understand how to harness this information properly. To make the most of this invaluable resource, you need to know how to access the records and convert the available information into meaningful and useful insights for yourself.

While there is no harm in doing this under the supervision of a formal guide or anyone else who has experience in this field, this is something you can do entirely on your own. Many people with proper certifications for teaching Akashic practices are not disciples of any master or guide. Instead, they have delved into the field of Akashic Records out of interest, and through trial and error and a lot of practice, they arrive at the stage where they can help other people. Many people rely on guides and masters to access the records on their behalf. However, this is not a necessary step, and it is recommended that you try to do this on your own.

When accessing the Akashic Records, you must keep in mind that you are dealing with energy and vibrations. It is not a cabinet or file of information where you can simply skip to the page you want to read and find what you are looking for. The Akashic Records are sensitive to who accesses them, how they are accessed, and when they are accessed. It's essential you understand that the Akashic Records are a store of information and not a database. It is information about the entire existence and not a fact book of the universe.

Moreover, someone can't use the Akashic Records merely to learn how much money they will make, what age they will die, or who their spouse will be. Think of the records in a similar way to talking to an extremely wise friend who has all the solutions to your problems. The input this wise friend gives you will vary due to circumstances and vary depending on what you need at that particular time.

For instance, one of the most common things that people seek the records is guidance in making major decisions in their lives.

Let's say you are looking for a job, and you access the Akashic Records daily for guidance. Also, assuming the entire job hunt takes you two months, and during this time, you access the records every day for guidance on what you should do to reach the job you want.

During the job hunt, you may make changes to your CV, change the way you dress, how you talk to people, the kinds of jobs you apply for, the salary, and a whole list of variables you constantly change to meet the employer's requirements. You also draw from the experience of job interviews. You may find that the Akashic Records tell you something different daily during this process. Sometimes it may be only slightly different from what you currently do. In other cases, it could be the complete opposite because, as the questioner, you too are changing. You aren't a static being, and therefore the answer to your question is also constantly changing. Moreover, the world around you, the world whose record the Akashic Records hold, is also changing. The Akashic Records consider this when creating an answer to your question.

In this way, several variables come into play, and many of these you have no control over. This example illustrates that the person asking the question also significantly impacts the answers received. Suppose you are asking the questions on your own. In that case, the Akashic Records are addressing you directly. They formulate an answer that will be the best answer to understand, considering your personality, perceptions, and mentality. If you have someone asking the questions on your behalf, the answer will be based on what the guide needs to understand and then relay the information to you. Therefore, the Akashic Records will give the guide an answer in a format the Akashic Records wanted to convey to you.

So, you can see that accessing the Akashic Records on your own is the best way to go. More importantly, it is a powerful skill to help you in many other areas of life with other advantages than just connecting you to the Akashic Records. To access and understand the Akashic Records, we will look at how you can alter your body and mind to change your vibrational energy. As previously discussed, the Akashic Records exist in a realm at a much higher vibrational energy than the physical dimension we exist in. To achieve this higher state, we need to alter our vibrational state.

What Is Vibrational Energy?

Whether living or nonliving, everything in the universe can create energy and exist at a certain vibrational energy level. Even things that are not visible or tangible, such as black holes, also emit energy, and they too have a unique vibration. Essentially, all things have a vibration which is the rhythm of their existence. We can see a few examples of naturally occurring rhythms within our bodies, such as the way we breathe, heart rate, and circadian rhythm. Modern scientific studies have also concluded that the rhythm in our bodies and the electric and magnetic waves produced by our bodies do impact the body it is emitted from – and things *near the body.*

The energy and vibration of every individual have an impact on the global population and even on the universe at large. While this may seem like a philosophical or metaphysical approach, there is a lot of science to back up these claims. Recent scientific research has been determined that even the molecules in our cells move and create a vibration in the body. While these vibrations are microscopic and even hard to detect with very powerful microscopes, their impact on our bodies and lives can be quite significant. The electromagnetic waves that this vibration of the cells creates impact how the body operates. If the cells in an organ are vibrating at a different frequency, it directly influences the physical performance of that organ and even influences our mental state. The vibration is a result of several different factors. For instance, the ambient temperature we are in can influence the vibration rate of molecules in our bodies. Similarly, even our mind, mood, and the people we are with influence the rate of vibration.

The Mind and Vibration

Countless studies have looked into the details of how our mental state, mood, and even our thoughts impact the body. One of the most important studies looked at the impact of media consumption on our mental state and the effect on the body. Two groups of young children were shown two separate movies. One movie was very happy and positive, and the other was a dark, scary, and sad story. Both groups had the level of antibodies in their saliva tested before and after the movies. As you would imagine, those exposed to the positive media showed an increase in antibodies after the movie. Those who watched the sad, scary movie showed a drastic reduction in the level of antibodies. This reaction is something you, too, may have noticed in life. When you feel low and blue, you tend to get sick more easily, whether it's a slightly sore throat or flu or a simple cold. When you feel positive about yourself, you don't have that many physical problems. Even if you come across a problem like an injury, it doesn't feel that bad, and you often recover much faster and better.

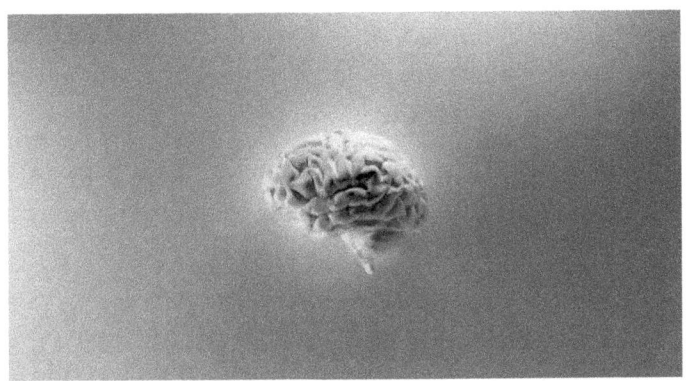

Similarly, you will have noticed that your heart rate goes up when you are stressed or anxious. This increase in heart rate is due to the body excreting the stress hormone that directly impacts your cardiovascular system. Additionally, certain sounds and music can also significantly sway the feelings and thoughts we experience. You will have noticed that the sound effects in a movie or a video greatly determine the overall feel of the scene. If you were to watch the same scene without the music, it would barely be as emotionally stirring as it is with the music.

Vibrational Energy and the Body

A growing pool of information suggests that our mind and body are interconnected and interdependent, but the energy we create in these situations impacts our overall being. For instance, if you are in a positive state of mind and your vibration level is high, you will notice that you physically feel different. You feel more positive, more able, stronger, and that you have more power with which you can attack life. On the contrary, a poor mental condition will often leave you feeling weak and crippled, and even though you are eating right and sleeping well, you feel lethargic, as if there is a strange burden on you.

Vibrational energy experts believe that positive energy is created when we feel positive emotions, such as happiness, love, a strong social connection, and a sense of achievement or accomplishment.

This positive energy vibrates at a higher rate. On the other hand, negative emotions of fear, stress, anxiety, and others, create negative energy that slows down our vibration.

Whether generated from electromagnetic waves, light, or sounds, vibrations of all kinds can promote good health in the body and the mind.

How to Improve Vibrational Energy

Luckily, we are in control of several things influencing our vibrational energy. Here are a few exercises and techniques you can adopt to get greater control of your vibrational energy and channel it towards the goals you want to achieve.

Do Yoga

Yoga can help you raise your vibrational energy because its poses allow you to search deeper in your mind, soul, and body, releasing stagnant, undesirable energy. Additionally, moving your body in a yoga flow allows your energy to vibrate. So, for instance, if you're feeling down, a vinyasa class can be very uplifting. A child's pose or other yin posture can help you reboot your body's system, raising your spirits.

Remedy Your Chakras

The next chapter covers the seven main chakras, the body's spiritual energy centers, in more depth. They're so important because they are where your main focus should be when it comes to raising your overall vibrations. Clearing any blockages in your chakras and ensuring the free flow of energy is necessary. Fortunately, there are numerous ways to practice reiki, use crystals and oils, and recite positive affirmations that can help unblock your energy centers.

Take Long Walks in Nature

There is no better way to lift your vibrational frequency than by immersing in nature's vast lands. Your energy will vibrate as you move your body and enjoy all the benefits that natural, fresh air and sunlight have to offer. Abandon your phone for the day and connect with the world around you. Listen to the chirping of the birds, focus on how the soft breeze on your skin, and observe how the sunlight falls on the trees around you. If possible, take your shoes off and feel the soil, grass, or sand with your feet. Stay for as long as your heart and soul desire. You will feel the energy shift within you.

Try a Sound Bath

Sound baths incorporate certain sounds and frequencies that stimulate a shift in the state of our brainwaves. This makes us more receptive and helps us feel more relaxed. If you don't have a specialized class in your area, you can search for online sound bath recordings to raise your vibrational energy.

Just Say No

Between running errands for your friend, helping out your co-worker with their tasks, and tending to your household chores, you end up feeling extremely tired and burned out. If this sounds like you, then the chances are that you constantly disregard your own needs while giving your all to others. Ignoring your personal wants and needs can decrease your positive vibrations. Although it sounds easier said than done, you need to practice saying no to what you really don't want to do. Once you get the hang of it, you'll feel your mood lighten and a weight lifted off your shoulders.

Positive Thoughts Only

Our thoughts directly impact our emotions. On the upside, our minds tend to make events and situations seem more stressful and negative than they really are. So, the next time you feel anxious or overwhelmed, take a moment to ponder whether the situation is really worth fretting about. You should also eliminate negative thoughts and look at the positive aspect of things.

Meditation

In a nutshell, meditation is the process through which you focus your mind on a particular thought and clear your mind of all unnecessary thoughts and concerns for a specified period. Different people approach this problem in different ways. Some people prefer to chant words or phrases, and others like to listen to music, while some prefer to sit in complete silence. Generally, there is no defined posture you have to be in to meditate, but the aim is to be completely relaxed and in a position you can hold for an extended period. You don't have to start with long meditation sessions. Even just meditating for five minutes is a great start, given that it is five minutes of quality meditation.

The most basic and possibly most effective approach to meditation is simply to focus on your breathing. You need to only think about how you are breathing, pay attention to every inhalation and exhalation, and try not to let your thoughts deviate from this one internal process that is happening. Meditation has been used for thousands of years, and it has been proven to impact the mental and physical condition of the practitioner explicitly.

It is particularly important when increasing your vibration level because by controlling your mind and thoughts, you can control the energy in your body and, subsequently, the created vibrational forces.

As you develop the capacity to sit for longer meditation sessions, you can shift your focus towards bringing positivity into your life. Some people do this by focusing on positive thoughts, like a mental image of something you deem positive or simply removing the negative thoughts. As you meditate, different thoughts will cross your mind. The aim is to develop enough control to not latch onto any thought but to let it pass through. Once you can do this, you can move on to focusing your energy on a particular thought.

Gratitude

Some people look at being grateful as a form of active meditation. It is something that you don't have to sit down to do.

Instead, do it in your mind throughout the day merely by staying mindful of what good things are happening in your life. More importantly, you don't have to wait for a positive scenario to be grateful for it or to be grateful for the life you have. There are many situations when we think that what is happening is wrong or it will be harmful, but in the long run, that same thing turns out to be a very positive and beneficial experience for us.

A powerful strategy you can use is making a list of things you are grateful for every day. You can do this as you wake up, later when you have time, or as the last thing when you go to bed. Making a list helps you focus on all the things you are consciously grateful for, and it also forces you to think of things you might not realize you are grateful for. In this way, you also manage yourself, your thoughts, and can streamline your mental processes. It also helps you get some control over your thoughts. Sometimes we are so mentally preoccupied with life, and we forget the things we are grateful for, and, in some cases, our thoughts get out of control. We also lose control of our energy and our vibrations with these thoughts. As the aim is to achieve a greater vibration level, being in control of your thoughts will help you stay on the right track to achieving a higher vibrational level.

Generosity

Being generous, sharing, donating, and even being generous with yourself has been shown to have a wide range of positive effects on people. Whether at a physical or mental level, nearly everyone has experienced the satisfaction of being generous. You get a unique feeling when you are genuinely generous, and it is done out of pure love for the other person. Being generous doesn't mean just giving to those in need or contributing to some philanthropic project, but even spending on the people you love is a form of generosity. Moreover, you can share a lot more than just your money. The time you give people, the honesty you give with, the ideas, and the genuine feelings you share are all part of being a generous person and open with the people around you. In many cases, being generous with those closest to you is more rewarding than helping strangers.

Diet and Lifestyle

The diet you consume and the lifestyle you lead have two effects. The main effect is that it directly impacts the body and the mind's condition. Eating healthy food with antioxidants, vitamins, and minerals with other vital nutrients our bodies need is key to helping the body perform. Exercising and staying in shape also helps the body significantly improve its performance and stay in a more positive mental state.

Another main benefit of eating healthy is that it impacts how we think about ourselves as individuals. Staying healthy, eating well, and exercising are personal challenges for nearly every person on the planet. When you do something that entails personal development, and it is challenging, it is incredibly satisfying and mentally stimulating, and it benefits us at a physical and a spiritual level. There is a huge rush of endorphins with all the health benefits, and it largely impacts our psychology and what we think of ourselves as people.

Overall, the effects are highly positive and help us fight off negative energy and turbocharge positive energy production. In return, we achieve a better vibrational level and get that much closer to achieving our goal of accessing the Akashic Records.

When you sit down to meditate and focus your attention on accessing the Akashic Records, you will sit in a space that increases your vibrational energy so that you can connect with that higher-tier power. When your base vibrational level is already high, it becomes that much easier to access a higher vibrational energy level. If you do a bit of all these things on a regular basis, you will have made marginal gains in many areas that contribute significantly toward increasing overall vibrational energy. More importantly, you have trained your body and mind to operate at the higher vibrational level and also developed better control in changing your vibration and energy.

Honesty

Being honest with oneself is one of the most radical ways to elevate vibrational energy. While we'd all rather think of ourselves as evolved, mature, healthy, enlightened, etc., honesty means coming to terms with one's own shortcomings. It also means admitting to hard truths about oneself, relationships, life goals, beliefs, and actions. By rooting out lies, getting rid of denial, and meeting yourself where you are and not where you hope to be, you can start loving yourself for who you are while making the changes you desire out of self-love.

More importantly, it will be much easier for you to figure out the path that best aligns with you when you're fully in tune with who you are.

Bear in mind that, while highly effective in raising vibrational energy, honesty is a very complex and exhausting process. It requires a gentle touch – but a firm one, nonetheless. It also requires perseverance and deep understanding, especially where forgiveness is necessary. As long as you root yourself in the infinite nature of love, no obstacle will stand in your way.

Chapter 5: Chakras 101

Energy can be difficult to understand. It flows through us in an infinite loop, and it takes a lot of work to keep things balanced. Our chakras are part of the energy system, but they also affect our emotional state and how we react to the world around us. This chapter talks about what chakra points are, why they're important for spiritual growth, and how you can use them in your life.

Why Are the Chakras Important?

When we talk about chakras, it's important to remember that they are part of the larger energy system. The seven major chakra points (seven being a very spiritual number) emit and receive different energies from other physical and metaphysical bodies. Working with these points regularly, you can clear out negative energy or blockages and keep yourself in a good state of mind.

The Chakras can be broken into three sections: the lower, middle, and higher chakras. Each controls certain aspects of our life and how we interact with those around us (even those not physically present). By working with each area regularly, you will push yourself forward into higher states of consciousness.

It may seem like a lot to work with so many points, but the truth is, you will only be working with one or two at any given time. Most people have seven chakra points. Although some are so inactive, they hardly serve many purposes for spiritual growth.

The History of Chakras

The chakra system has been around for a long time. Some people believe that it can be traced back to ancient Indian teachings, but we know now that the seven major points have their roots in the Vedas, dating back to the 1000 BC eras. The word "chakra" means "wheel" in Sanskrit, and the seven major points are often represented as swirling orbs of energy emitting different colors.

Each chakra has a unique frequency and vibration. When they are in balance, we operate at our full potential. However, when one or more chakra points become blocked, it can cause all sorts of problems in our lives. Physical health issues, emotional instability, and even spiritual stagnation can result.

Flow of Energy

The flow of energy through the chakra points is an important part of our existence. If we don't have enough energy flowing from one area to another, there will be major problems dealing with day-to-day life and even spiritual growth.

The easiest way to think of the energy flow is as a circle. Each chakra point has its own energy that affects us differently, depending on what it "tells" our body and mind.

The flow of energy through each chakra point works in a specific order. This is why it's crucial to keep them balanced and open and why blocking one has such adverse effects on our emotional state.

Each chakra is associated with several things, including our physical and emotional health, spiritual growth, and how we interact with the world around us. We'll go into more detail about each one in a bit, but for now, it's important to understand that these points are vitally imperative for our overall well-being.

Every chakra also has a number, color, and a particular position in the spine.

1. The Root Chakra

The Root Chakra can be found at the base of the spine and is responsible for our sense of grounding and connection to the physical world. This chakra is all about survival and keeping us safe. When it's in balance, we feel secure, safe, and stable. We're able to handle stress better and don't get overwhelmed as easily.

Location: The base of the spine

Color: Red

Stands For: Stability and survival

A blocked chakra in this area can manifest as problems with our feet, legs, colon, and bladder. We may also feel a lack of connection to the earth or have difficulty staying grounded. Feelings of insecurity and fear are also common.

The Root Chakra is responsible for our sense of grounding and connection to the physical world. This chakra is all about survival and keeping us safe. When it's in balance, we feel secure, safe, stable, and able to handle stress better; we don't get overwhelmed as easily.

Opening the Root Chakra

To open this chakra, you need to do a few things.

First of all, it's essential to feel your connection with the earth. The more in touch we are with nature and our physicality, the easier this will become. While meditation can help us reach a state where we feel more rooted, it's important to take time each day for activities that make us feel grounded.

Some people find connectivity through yoga and exercise. Stomping your feet, Kundalini Yoga, and the Bridge Pose are some ways to open your lower spine. Eating red-colored foods like apples, tomatoes, and beets is an excellent way to balance the Root Chakra.

2. The Sacral Chakra

The Sacral Chakra is located in the lower abdomen and is responsible for our emotions, creativity, and sexuality. This chakra is all about pleasure and how we experience life. When it's in balance, we enjoy life and find joy in everyday experiences. We're also more creative and expressive.

Location: Lower abdomen

Color: Orange

Stands For: Creativity, expression, emotions, and pleasure. A blocked chakra in this area can cause problems with the reproductive organs, kidneys, and liver. We may also feel disconnected from our emotions or have a hard time expressing ourselves creatively. Depression is also common when this point becomes unbalanced.

The Sacral Chakra is responsible for our emotions, creativity, and sexuality. This chakra is all about pleasure and how we experience life. When it's in balance, we enjoy life and find joy in everyday experiences. We're also more creative and expressive.

Opening the Sacral Chakra

To open this chakra, think about things that bring you pleasure and joy. It can be as simple as enjoying a cup of coffee or tea to something more extravagant like a vacation. The goal is to find activities that help us connect with our creativity and emotions to live life fully without feeling overwhelmed by negativity.

A great way to open the Sacral Chakra is by doing Yoga poses like Camel Pose, Child's Pose, and Fish Pose. Eating orange foods or food with an orange hue can also help balance this chakra.

3. The Solar Plexus Chakra

The Solar Plexus chakra is located in the stomach and is responsible for our personal power, self-esteem, and how we see ourselves. This chakra is all about standing up for what you believe in, no matter what anyone else says or thinks. You can follow your path and feel comfortable in your skin when it's open.

Location: Stomach

Color: Yellow

Stands For: Personal power, self-esteem, finding our voice. A blocked chakra here can lead to digestive issues like stomach ulcers or other problems with the liver, gallbladder, and spleen. We may also feel like we're not good enough or have low self-esteem. We may be afraid to speak up for ourselves or afraid to take risks.

Exercises like Yoga and Tai Chi can help to open the Solar Plexus Chakra. It's also important to eat yellow foods or have a yellow hue. Bananas, pineapple, and corn are all great examples. Teas like chamomile, ginger, and lavender can also help to open this chakra.

4. The Heart Chakra

The heart chakra can be found in the center of the chest and is responsible for our relationships with others, both romantic and platonic. This chakra is all about love, compassion, and forgiveness.

When it's open, we have healthy relationships with others and can give and receive love freely.

Location: Center of chest

Color: Green

Stands For: Love, compassion, forgiveness. A blocked chakra in this area can lead to heart disease, respiratory issues, and joint pain. We may also have difficulty forgiving others or feel resentment towards them. The Heart Chakra is about relationships, so it's important to focus on activities that help us connect with others. Things like meditation, volunteering, and spending time in nature help open this chakra. Eating green foods or having a green hue is also beneficial. Green leafy vegetables, cucumbers, and kiwi fruit are great examples. Teas like peppermint, lavender, and chamomile are suitable.

5. The Throat Chakra

The throat chakra is located in the neck and deals with verbal and nonverbal communication. This chakra is about speaking our truth without fear of judgment or repercussion. Being open here allows us to communicate clearly and honestly, which can help us achieve goals more efficiently by allowing others to support us.

Location: Neck, throat area

Color: Blue or turquoise

Stands For: This chakra is all about expressing ourselves through the spoken and written word and communicating with others without fear of judgment or repercussion. When this chakra is open, you can speak up for yourself and easily share your thoughts and ideas. You may also find that you're a more effective leader as others are likely to follow your lead.

Singing, chanting, shoulder stands, and Yoga poses that open the chest area help open this chakra. Teas like peppermint, lavender, and chamomile are great for throat health, so you may want to drink these before bed or first thing in the morning if your energy is low. Foods with blue hues like berries and grapes are also beneficial.

6. The Third Eye Chakra

The third eye chakra is located in the center of your forehead and deals with intuition, perception, insight, learning, and memory. This chakra lets you know what's important to focus on so you can give appropriate attention to it while letting go of what fails to serve a purpose.

Location: Center of the forehead, between the eyebrows

Color: Indigo or deep blue-violet

Stands For: Intuition, perception, insight, and learning are all parts of this chakra. When it's open, you make connections more easily, helping with your memory and learning new things. You may also find that you're more in tune with your intuition and gut feelings, which help you make better decisions.

This chakra is all about focus and concentration, so activities like meditation, yoga, and focusing on the breath are very helpful in opening it up. Eating foods with an indigo hue, like blueberries, plums, and eggplant, are great for this chakra. Teas like lavender or jasmine can also be beneficial.

7. The Crown Chakra

The crown chakra is at the top of your head and is responsible for your connection to the divine. This chakra is all about letting go of ego and self-centeredness to connect with something larger than ourselves. When it's open, we see things from a higher perspective and focus on what's genuinely important in life.

Location: Top of the head, crown area

Color: Violet or white (seen as gold when open)

Stands For: This chakra is all about letting go of ego and self-centeredness to connect with something larger than ourselves.

When it's open, we can see things from a higher perspective and focus on what's truly important in life.

This chakra is all about the divine, so activities like meditation, prayer, or any practice that brings you closer to your spiritual side will help open it up. Running and meditation are two great activities that can help open the crown chakra. Eating foods with a violet hue, like blackberries, plums, and eggplant, are great for this chakra. Teas like lavender or jasmine can also be beneficial.

Aligning the Chakras to Access the Akashic Records

Now that we've gone over the seven main chakras, let's talk about how aligning them helps us access the Akashic Records.

The first step is to set your intention. We can harness the energy of our chakras by setting an intention with a strong sense of will and desire.

Next, move on to visualization, which is when you see yourself at that moment where you access the Akashic Records. Some people do this best by visualizing themselves in the Akashic library, and others like to imagine an energy portal opening up. How you choose to get there doesn't matter as long as it works for you.

Lastly, do your best not to judge or compare what is happening during this process because everything will happen in its own time and way. Like any other spiritual practice, it's important to have patience and let go of the need for control.

Take the quiz below to determine what you should work on first.

Find Out Which of Your Chakras Needs Balancing

Q1. Which color does not appeal to you at all?

    a) Red

    b) Orange

    c) Yellow

    d) Green

    e) Blue

    f) Indigo

    g) Violet

Q2. Which of the following qualities do you wish you had?

    a) Grounded

    b) Joyful

    c) Confident

    d) Loving

    e) Expressive

    f) Wise

    g) Connected

Q3. Which beverage do you like the most?

    a) Coffee

    b) Milk

    c) Water

    d) Soda pop

    e) Tea with lemon or honey

    f) Alcoholic Beverages

    g) Fresh Juices

Q4. Do you feel like you have nothing to look forward to in life?

    a) No; I look forward to new experiences all the time

    b) Somewhat, but not as much as I used to

    c) Not at all; every day is a new adventure

    d) Only when something major is happening

    e) Rarely; most of the time, I feel like there's something to look forward to

    f) Almost never; I feel like life is passing me by

Q5. Which of the following gemstones would you love to wear?

    a) Diamond

    b) Ruby

    c) Quartz

    d) Amethyst

    e) Onyx

    f) Pearls

Q6. Would you call yourself an honest person?

    a) Yes, I always tell the truth

    b) Mostly I tell the truth, but there are a few things I hold back

    c) No, sometimes I bend the truth to fit my needs

    d) It depends on the situation

    e) Rarely; honesty is not really one of my virtues

Q7. Which of the following flowers is your favorite?

    a) Rose

    b) Orchid

    c) Lily

    d) Sunflower

    e) Daisy

f) Chrysanthemum

Q8. Do you like to be alone or around people?

a) Alone - I enjoy my own company and find it relaxing to be by myself sometimes

b) Around People - I prefer to be around my friends and family

c) Both - I enjoy being alone and with others, but also find it relaxing to sometimes just sit in silence for a while

Q9. Do you find it difficult to focus on one task at a time?

a) No, I can focus on anything that I need to

b) It depends on the task, some things are easy to focus on, and others are more difficult

c) Yes, it takes me a while to really get into something and stay focused

Q10. Which of the following scents is most appealing to you?

a) Jasmine

b) Lavender

c) Vanilla

d) Peppermint

e) Cinnamon

f) Pineapple

Q11. Are you a patient person?

a) Yes, I am very patient and can wait for things to happen in their own time

b) Mostly, but there are times when I get impatient and want things to happen now

c) No, I like to see results quickly and am not very good at waiting for things

Q12. Are you comfortable talking about your emotions?

a) Yes, I don't mind talking about anything and am always up for a good talk

b) Sometimes – it depends on the subject, but sometimes things are hard to discuss

c) No – It's not that I'm unwilling. There aren't many people who can understand me or relate to what I'm going through

Q13. Do you like to create change in your life?

a) Yes, I like to be in control of my life and make changes when needed

b) Somewhat – I like some change but not too much at once

c) No, I prefer things to stay the same most of the time

d) It depends on what kind of change we're talking about. For example, I like to change my hair color maybe once a month

Q14. Which part of your body causes you the most discomfort?

a) adrenal, kidney, feet, knees, hips

b) ovaries, hormonal imbalance

c) digestive system

d) lungs, circulation, heart, immune system

e) throat, thyroid, mouth, teeth, jaw, ears (ENT system)

f) pituitary, eyes, sinuses, headaches

g) Spinal gland, insomnia, nerves (anxiety)

Q15. Are you afraid of moving on with life?

a) No, I am always looking for new opportunities and experiences

b) Somewhat – I'm not afraid of moving on, but it's something that I have to think about carefully

c) Yes, I'm scared of what might happen if I let go of the past

d) It depends on what "Moving On" means

e) Yes, I want to move on, but people and things are holding me back from doing that

f) No, I am always moving forward in life no matter what happens in the past or present

g) Sometimes – it depends on how much progress I've made balancing my "past," "present," and "future."

Q16. Are you a sympathetic person?

a. Yes, I feel other people's pain and am always there to help

b. Somewhat – I can be sympathetic at times, but it depends on the person

c. No, I don't care about others' feelings - I have my own problems to deal with

d. Sometimes – it depends on the person and why they are feeling a certain way, and what kind of help they want from me

e. It depends on what "Sympathetic" means

f. No, most people's pain is their problem, not mine

g. Yes, I always feel bad for people who are in a tough situation and want to help them in any way that I can

Q17. Do you like to take risks?

a) Yes, I love trying new things and taking risks

b) Somewhat – I like some risks but not too many at once

c) No, I don't enjoy doing things that might have a chance of failure

d) It depends on what kind of risks we're talking about

e) Yes, but only if the risk has a big enough reward for me, and I am sure that it will work out well

f) No, there are so many risks involved in taking chances with your life or future. Why would you ever want to take those kinds of unnecessary risks?

g) It depends on the risk involved - some risks are worth taking, and others aren't

Q18. Do you get defensive easily?

a) No, I'm not very sensitive to criticism and can take it in my stride

b) Yes, but only if the person criticizing me is someone that I respect or care about

c) Yes, I get very defensive because people will say anything to try and bring me down

d) It depends on the circumstances - sometimes I can take criticism well, but other times not so much

e) No, in general, I'm a pretty easy-going person who just wants to have fun with other people and doesn't get too upset about what others say

f) I can be defensive, but only because it's important for me to stick up for myself when other people put me down or judge me unfairly

g) The opinions of other people don't bother me - if they have nothing nice to say, then they shouldn't say anything at all

Answers:

Mostly As: Your Root Chakra needs balancing.

Mostly Bs: Your Sacral Chakra needs balancing.

Mostly Cs, Ds, or Es: Your Solar Plexus Chakra needs balancing.

Mostly Fs or Gs: Your Heart Chakra needs balancing.

Feelings of insecurity, fear, and anxiety are the symptoms of an imbalanced Heart Chakra.

Inability to focus, impatience, and difficulty discussing emotions are symptoms of an imbalanced Solar Plexus Chakra.

Chakras are energy centers in your body that affect everything from emotional well-being to physical health, so it's essential to understand them for a holistic approach to living. This knowledge will help you take steps towards becoming more grounded and centering yourself daily. You might want to incorporate some or all of these exercises into your yoga routine if you already practice. If not, they could be an excellent way to get started. Lastly, while there's no substitute for experience when balancing your energies through meditation, visualization, breathing techniques, or other practices drawn from ancient traditions like Yoga or Chinese Medicine, it's always helpful to have a teacher you can talk to if you notice anything out of the ordinary.

Like chakras, breathing is a vital part of our everyday lives, and we need to function at optimal levels. It's imperative that all people practice proper breathing techniques daily, even when it seems easy or natural. Ultimately, breathing is an excellent way to work with the chakras and achieve a more balanced state of being.

Chapter 6: Unblocking the Chakras

The chakras represent the energy centers in our bodies located along the spine. These energy centers start at the base of the spine and end at the crown of the head. Each corresponds to a cluster of nerves, specific organs, and other points of the body where energy is used. Many believe there could be over 100 different chakras in our bodies, but the term chakra typically refers to the seven main centers affecting our energy balance. These bundles collect and conduct vital energy. The energy flow needs to be uninterrupted for the body to function optimally, which is only possible when the chakras are open. If they are blocked, the chakras cannot conduct your energy properly, and your body and mind will suffer the consequences. This chapter explores the seven major chakras more closely, along with symptoms of their blockage. It also discusses possible solutions for unblocking them, allowing you to focus your energy positively.

The Importance of the Chakras

Each of the seven major chakras affects our well-being, which is why they are distinguished by a specific name, number, color, and meaning. Their location and role in our health are precisely determined, allowing us to discover the root of our health issues. While exploring the chakras, you discover that their energy corresponds to different emotions. The feeling that resonates with each cluster of energy can come from physical and mental sources and will always depend on individual circumstances. Due to the ongoing processes in your body, the emotions resonating in a chakra can change daily. However, sometimes a negative feeling prevails over an extended period, indicating that the chakra is blocked. The blockages in the chakra system are quite common, and, fortunately, there is a treatment for most.

While the seven chakras are identical in each human being, their blockage is often caused by different factors. Moreover, one person may experience physical or mental symptoms induced by a blockage in one organ. In contrast, another will experience the same symptoms related to a different issue because the chakras are affected by external environmental factors and internally. Each of us is subjected to stress in many different ways in our day-to-day life.

Whether we face professional or personal challenges, our bodies react to them differently. Additionally, our bodies undergo many changes as we age, such as decreased energy flow. All this affects our chakras and blocks them from time to time.

Fortunately, there are many ways to unblock your chakras and restore the balance in your energy flow. The choices are vast and vary from establishing a healthier lifestyle to using healing crystals and oils. However, it's important to note that your success in correcting your chakra imbalance will depend on your willingness to put in the required effort. These techniques have been used successfully for centuries. But, for them to work for you, you must be ready to explore your inner nature and your environment.

Unblocking the Seven Major Chakras

1. The Root Chakra

Location: At the base of your spine

Color: Red

Meaning: Stability, grounding, and identity

As its name suggests, the root chakra helps you stay grounded despite life's challenges. Moreover, this center can help you establish the foundation for your life by providing you with a sense of security. If blocked, this chakra will manifest in physical symptoms, such as digestive problems, bladder issues, and arthritis. The emotional consequences of a closed root chakra are insecurity over your well-being, depression, anxiety, and low self-esteem. You may also feel disconnected from your roots and environment. When open, you have an absolute sense of security in your future while feeling grounded at the same time.

Here is how to unblock the root chakra:

- **With Food:** Red-colored food, such as tomatoes, beets, chilies, radish, and strawberries, works best for unblocking this center. Consuming carrots and other root vegetables may also help.

- **Through Yoga:** The child's pose, the bridge, standing forward, and the reclining angle poses all have great grounding effects, meaning they can help you realign with your roots.

- **With Crystals:** Red and black colored crystals, such as ruby, red jasper, or obsidian, connect with this chakra the best. You can place them on the soles of your feet or lower back while lying on your stomach.

- **Using Oils:** To unblock the root chakra, you can massage with it nutmeg oil. Patchouli is excellent for lowering overly high energy levels, and Bergamot oil helps restore the balance in this center.

- **Using Positive Affirmations:** By repeating positive affirmations about safety, you will relate more to your environment, helping you break the habits that don't allow you to feel safe.

- **Practicing Meditation:** People with root chakra issues may find it hard to meditate in a sitting position. If this is the case, you can always try meditation while walking. It will require you to walk barefoot on sand, grass, or dirt to feel more connected to your roots.

2. The Sacral Chakra

Location: Below your belly button

Color: Orange

Meaning: Creativity and pleasure

This chakra determines how you express your emotions and relate to other people's feelings. It's also responsible for supplying you with creative energy that you can use to explore relationships and sexuality. When the sacral chakra is blocked, you may experience physical symptoms, such as fatigue, lower back pain, sexual dysfunction, and infections in the genital area. The inability to feel joy and pleasure in your relationship or be creative may also occur. In contrast, when the sacral chakra is open, you feel energized to create and dedicated to your relationships sexually and emotionally.

Here is how to unblock the sacral chakra:

- **Through Food:** Oranges, pumpkins, mangoes, honey, and other orange-colored food help open this energy center.

- **Through Yoga:** Poses that help open your body will promote exploring sexuality and creativity. These are the cobra, the pigeon, the frog, and the hip opener postures.

- **With Crystals:** Due to their orange or red color, crystals like garnet, orange calcite, bloodstone, and carnelian can open this chakra. Put them on your body a little below your navel while resting.

- **Using Oils:** Massaging spicy cardamom oil will open up the chakra, neroli may calm its energy, while sweet orange will restore its balance.

- **Using Positive Affirmations:** Repeating affirmations about creativity sensuality help restore your faith in these skills. You can even use them to spice up your relationship.

- **Practicing Meditation:** Creativity comes from your ability to go with the flow. The best way to practice this is via meditation near water. You can sit by it, go in, or even swim slowly. They all help you relax and get creative.

3. The Solar Plexus Chakra

Location: Upper abdominal area

Color: Yellow

Meaning: Confidence and self-esteem

The solar plexus chakra is responsible for raising your confidence levels and helps you take control of your life. When it's blocked, you have diminished self-esteem, feel worthless, anxious, and powerless to do anything. The blockage of this center may also show up as indigestion, heartburn, ulcers, and eating disorders. By unblocking it, you can empower yourself with confidence to take charge of your life and live it the way you want to.

You can unblock the solar plexus chakra through the following methods:

- **Through Food**: Fresh, yellow-colored food, such as corn, bananas, apricots, and pineapple, is best for opening the chakra.

- **Through Yoga:** Poses like the bow, the boar, the warrior, or backbends strengthen your core and help restore the healthy energy flow to this chakra.

- **With Crystals:** Gold or yellow crystals, such as citrine, gold tiger's eye, yellow quartz, and yellow calcite can unblock this chakra. Place them around your solar plexus on your abdomen while relaxing, or wear them as jewelry throughout the day.

- **Using Oils:** To unblock this chakra, you can massage your stomach with eucalyptus oil. You can use citrus essential oil to restore the energy balance and helichrysum to lower its levels.

- **Using Positive Affirmations**: By repeating affirmations about personal power, you can take control over your life. As you repeat the positive thoughts about what you can do to improve your life, you will slowly start believing them.

- **Practicing Meditation:** Use breathing and other meditation techniques to reach into yourself and discover what caused your low self-esteem. Whether it was caused by upbringing or any other emotional trauma, the balance in your solar plexus chakra is often lost far earlier than the symptoms appear. Uncovering the cause may help restore it.

4. The Heart Chakra

Location: In the center of your chest

Color: Green

Meaning: Compassion, love, and nurturing

This chakra, located near your heart, naturally has an enormous impact on developing emotions, such as love, compassion, and empathy. The blockage of the heart chakra causes circulatory and pulmonary problems. It may also lead to weight gain, which often occurs due to other physical and emotional issues. The latter include the inability to feel love, especially for yourself, and you always put others first. You may also find it challenging to let go past grievances, connect to others, or be confident about your future. Restoring this energy center will make you feel more secure in connecting with yourself and others. In addition, the heart chakra is located in the middle of the seven, meaning its healthy function maintains the energy flow between the others.

You can unblock the heart chakra in the following ways:

- **Through Food:** To unlock this chakra, you must consume green products, such as spinach, broccoli, Brussels sprouts, kale, lettuce, and green lentils.

- **Through Yoga:** Poses like shoulder stretches, backbends, the eagle, or the camel pose may help strengthen your core, ribcage, and arms resulting in a healthier function of the heart and lungs.

- **With Crystals:** Green crystals, such as jade, green calcite, and emerald, work the best on this chakra, but you can also use pink quartz to encourage positive feelings. Place a crystal on the center of your chest while lying still. You can also wear them as a necklace during the day.

- **Using Oils:** Massaging palmarosa oil on your breastbone is the most effective for unblocking the heart chakra. Lavender helps with overactive energy, while geranium in the middle of the back will keep the heart center functioning properly.

- **Using Positive Affirmations:** You can restore your ability to give and receive love and compassion by repeating affirmations related to emotional healing.

- **Practicing Meditation:** Breathing techniques often used in meditation can help you to relax and open up your soul to emotions. It also allows you to focus on yourself more, which you may find uncomfortable at first. However, over time, you will learn the benefits of this practice.

5. The Throat Chakra

Location: In the throat

Color: Blue

Meaning: Communication

The throat chakra mainly affects your ability to express yourself verbally, but its effects also extend to physical symptoms. The root of most problems related to mouth and throat areas, such as the vocal cords, the thyroid, the teeth, and the gums, are found in this chakra. Furthermore, the blockage of this energy center can result in various verbal communication issues. These can go from merely being dishonest to being shy and unable to speak your mind to the need to dominate conversations and speak without thinking. On the other hand, when your throat chakra is open, you speak confidently and articulate your thoughts properly. You can also listen to your conversation partners and understand their points of view.

Ways to unblock your throat chakra:

- **Through Food:** Eating fresh, colorful food, such as wheatgrass, dragon fruit, ginseng, blackberries, and blueberries, may help unblock the energy.

- **Through Yoga:** Recommended positions for this issue are shoulder stand, fish pose, plow pose, and bridge pose. These all strengthen the neck area, helping to restore your chakra.

- **With Crystals:** Wearing jewelry with blue healing crystals around your neck will have a powerful effect on this chakra. Look for necklaces with angelite, sodalite, turquoise, or blue calcite, and wear them all day until your issue is resolved.

- **Using Oils:** Spraying different oils on your neck will have diverse effects. For example, coriander oil will promote healthy energy flow, lemon will restore a blocked chakra, and vanilla will balance your energy.

- **Using Positive Affirmations:** To unblock this chakra, repeat several different affirmations that refer to communication and authenticity. You may also press on about the importance of inner truth. These will get you in the right direction for communicating with others.

- **Practicing Meditation:** Through meditation techniques, you can learn to focus your mind, which will come in handy in your day-to-day communication. Even a couple of quiet minutes a day will make you realize how important it is to focus on the essence. You will also connect to your inner self, which will help open the throat chakra.

6. The Third Eye Chakra

Location: Between your eyes

Color: Indigo

Meaning: Imagination and intuition

Your third eye is responsible for imagery, imagination, and, most importantly, for your intuition. The blockage of this chakra causes symptoms indicating issues with your brain and mind. Physical symptoms include vision and hearing problems, headaches, confusion, and dizziness. You may have trouble listening to your gut instinct and be unable to make decisions. Or, you refuse to listen to your intuition because you think you already know it all. Unblocking the third eye will resolve this, letting you get in touch with your instincts and see the actual reality.

Here are some ways to unblock the third eye chakra

- **Through Food:** Consuming, purple-colored food, such as plums, eggplants, purple lettuce, purple carrots, and grapes, can contribute to restoring the energy in this region.

- **Through Yoga:** Supported forward bends can help you visualize positive outcomes and affirm them by making the imagery more vivid.

- **With Crystals**: Lie down for a couple of minutes a day with a purple or blue crystal on your forehead in between your eyes just above the bridge of your nose. Sapphire, amethyst, sugilite, and lapis lazuli work best for clearing the pathways in this region.

- **Using Oils:** By applying rosemary essential oil to your forehead between your eyes and just above 5he nose, you can unblock this chakra. German chamomile oil suits the overworked energy in this center, while sandalwood will restore its balance.

- **Using Positive Affirmations**: Repeating affirmations related to awareness and intuition can help open up your third eye and give you a little more insight into the things happening around you.

- **Practicing Meditation:** Through mindful breathing techniques in meditation, you can become more focused on your instincts. As you relax and breathe, your thoughts influenced by your environment will be stilled, you will stop relying on them, and use your gut instinct instead.

7. The Crown Chakra

Location: At the top of your head

Color: Violet

Meaning: Intelligence and awareness

The crown chakra represents your tool for forming spiritual connections and, through them, help you determine your life purpose. Its location on the head means it's affecting the brain and the spine, often causing migraines, dizziness, and headaches. However, as this chakra is connected to all the other energy clusters in the body, its blockage can also result in other physical symptoms. An impaired crown chakra can cause narrow-mindedness, skepticism, and stubbornness when it affects your spirit. You may also feel lost and unable to connect to the spiritual world or fully embrace your beliefs. Unblocking this chakra often leads to powerful spiritual enlightenment and finding one's purpose. An open crown chakra will also help keep all the others open, ensuring proper energy flow through the entire body.

Here is how to unblock the crown chakra:

- **Through Food:** Since the blockage of this energy center can cause problems with the others and vice versa, eating anything could make everything worse. For this reason, the best solution for issues with the crown chakra is fasting with just fluids for about 48 hours. Typically, after this time, all your organs will be cleaned, and all the pathways of energy flow will clear.

- **Through Yoga:** Any yoga pose that affects the other energy centers will affect this one, too. The combination of poses used for the other six major chakras seems to be the most helpful with unblocking this one.

- **With Crystals:** Look for purple or white crystals, and place them on the top of your head. The best way to do this is when meditating, but you can also do it while sitting still for at least a couple of minutes. Amethyst, selenite, moonstone, diamonds, and clear quartz are excellent for restoring this chakra.

- **Using Oils:** Chakra oils work best for the crown chakra when inhaled. Use frankincense in a diffuser to balance the chakra, neroli to calm the energy, or sweet lavandin to unblock it.

- **Using Positive Affirmations:** Repeating positive affirmations that refer to spirituality will enlighten your soul while also opening up your crown chakra at the same time.

- **Practicing Meditation:** It allows you to focus your thoughts. Meditation can be a great way to reconnect with your inner self. Focusing on your breathing will ensure that your mind quietens enough so you can observe your thoughts rather than be consumed by them. While you may find it difficult to let thoughts go, doing it will eventually enable you to connect to your divine self.

While all these techniques will work perfectly for opening the individual chakras, you must remember that all of these points are connected. Sometimes, the imbalance in one chakra will also affect the other chakras. In this case, fixing the one won't be enough to restore the balance in your body. For you to become a truly healthy and happy individual, all your chakras need to be open. You must pay attention to any signs your body and mind show you and react as soon as you notice any changes to achieve this.

Last but not least, on your journey towards unblocking your chakras, remember that the road won't be straightforward. You may have to unblock a chakra more than once, and you may find it easier to unblock certain chakras than others. That is why patience is key, and once again, don't forget to be gentle with yourself. Don't get stuck in the negative cycle of blame every time you face a blockage or struggle too hard. Just like a flower takes time to bloom, you too will take time.

Chapter 7: Cleansing Your Mind

Accessing your Akashic Records is not as complicated as you may think. The trick is to clear your mind by channeling all the negative thoughts and energy away from your mind, body, and soul. Practice a few meditative exercises to declutter your mind and create a space to access information in your subconscious mind.

You can try different techniques to calm your mind and get rid of negative energy. Many cultures use meditation to tune with their spirituality or to release any causes of stress in their lives. To access your Akashic Records, your mind needs to be opened to accept the information you will receive from your subconscious mind. You can try several meditative practices to learn which one you are most comfortable with. We will outline a few methods on how to meditate to clear your mind. This chapter discusses how you can access Akashic Records by cleansing your mind.

Perspective Shifting

Before we delve deeper into heavier mind-cleansing techniques and methods, it's important for you to learn how to change the way you view negative thoughts. Most of us grow up classifying thoughts into negative and positive. While this is completely normal, it's not entirely healthy as it creates the habit of rejecting negative thoughts, which is very similar to sweeping dust under the rug. Granted, you won't see the dust, but the room will still be dirty.

Rejecting negative thoughts, blocking them, or distracting yourself from them may make you not think of them, but they'll still be there. They will affect your actions, mood, chakras, and in the end, they will come out.

In order to truly cleanse your mind, you need to learn how to accept your thoughts without getting caught up in what you think of them (negative/positive). Despite how scary this may seem, the fact is, once you're able to ground yourself, you'll be able to sit with your thoughts. Once you're able to sit with your thoughts, you can then learn how to observe them with understanding and compassion without engaging them.

You are not your thoughts. As long as you keep this in mind, you'll be able to channel the negative thoughts away and keep a clear mind.

Spiritual Meditation

Many religions involve meditation through prayer. People recite certain prayers from their sacred books to be in touch with God or a higher power. Religious people usually practice spiritual meditation or prayers at home or in a place of worship. However, you don't have to follow a religion to practice spiritual meditation. The purpose of meditation is to clear your mind and soul from any negative traces, meaning you can consider meditation as spiritual.

- How you practice spiritual meditation is entirely up to your own preferences. There is no particular way or steps you have to follow. Find a practice that feels right to you. Here are a few steps you can follow to practice spiritual meditation:
- First, sit as comfortably as you can in a quiet room in your house. You can put a thick blanket or pillow beneath you, so you don't have to interrupt your meditation session because your legs are numb.
- Cross your legs and place your hands comfortably on your knees, or place your right hand on your heart and the other beneath your belly button. Try whichever position feels most natural to you.
- You may feel that you can't empty your mind from its rushing thoughts. The best way is to exhale every thought as if you are pushing it away from your body.
- Focus on your breathing pattern, in and out. Concentrate on the sounds of your breath and feel how your body moves with each breath that you take.
- As you breathe in, feel your shoulders lifting and your back straightening a bit more. Feel the air going into your lungs and into each living cell in your body.

- As you breathe out, feel your shoulders relaxing and keep your posture. Don't allow your back to slouch. Sitting up straight helps you to breathe easier.

- Now, try to see brightness shining from within your soul. Imagine what your inner colors look like and feel the different heat sensations of each color.

- Follow this brightness as you get acquainted with its movements across your body. See how it is transferred from your body to the sky above you to connect with a higher power.

- Be open to the light you see and stay there as long as you like. When you feel ready, allow the brightness to return to your body.

- Flex your fingers and toes, uncross your legs, and slowly get back to your reality. Open your eyes gradually and get up when you feel ready. You will feel exhilarated from the whole experience.

Spiritual meditation is recommended to be practiced in the morning and before going to bed. You can also practice any time of day if you want to. If you meditate in the morning, write down what you want to get out of the meditative practice. Set your mind with the intention of clearing your head and opening up your mind to new realms. If you meditate before going to bed, make sure you have no distractions around you. Remove any electronic devices from your bedside, and don't check your phone after your meditative session to ensure a good night's sleep.

Reiki

Reiki is a Japanese therapy that is considered an alternative or complementary medicinal practice. It is energy healing by removing any blocks in your body to allow a smooth energy flow. The term refers to the vital energy that flows in everything around us.

Practicing Reiki can help you to clear your mind and access your Akashic Records more easily.

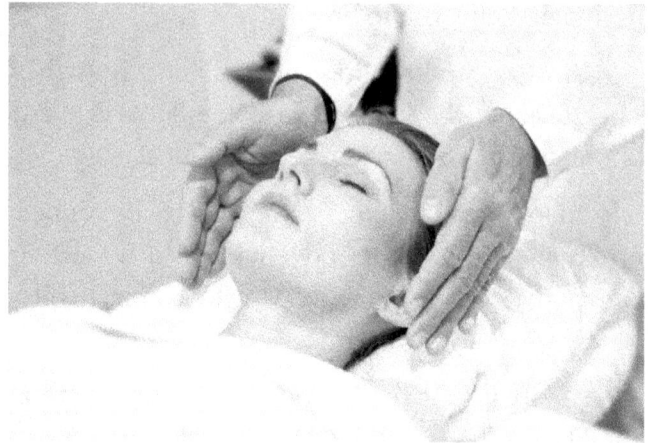

Reiki practitioners believe that blocked energy causes a wide range of health problems physically and mentally. It is also believed to cause misfortune, and the whole purpose of this therapy is to restore your inner balance to ensure vitality and prosperity. To prepare yourself for a reiki session, follow these steps:

- First, you have to believe in the concept of reiki which is that vital energy flows through all living things.

- You can practice a self-treatment session at home for 20 minutes in the morning and evening. Practicing twice a day is the standard, and you can increase the time of each session up to an hour.

- Choose a quiet room in your house away from any distractions; stipulate this area in your home for reiki sessions. The positions are more flexible in reiki than meditation as you can perform the session sitting on a chair or couch or even lying down on your bed. You can also sit or lie on the floor if you prefer.

- Play relaxing music if it helps you get in the mood for a therapy session. You can find reiki-related music online to play during your session.

- Make sure you are comfortable by lying or sitting on a pillow, taking off your shoes, and covering your feet with a blanket for comfort.

- Close your eyes and focus on your breathing until you achieve a rhythmic pattern.

Once you get into a relaxed state, you are ready to start the treatment. Follow these steps in the same order, and each position should be held for two minutes to complete a 20-minute session.

- Place your hands together as if you are praying. They should be right under your chin in the middle of your chest. Keep focusing on breathing in and out in a rhythmic pattern.

- Touch the top of your head on the sides with both your hands. Concentrate on how your hand feels on your head as you breathe in and out. Feel the comfort as it seeps through your hands onto your head.

- Cover your eyes with both your hands as you continue breathing in the same pattern. Avoid covering your nose in this exercise to allow easier breathing. Concentrate on your hand position on your eyes. Feel the heat energy coming out of your palms onto your eyes. Relax your muscles on your cheeks, forehead, and eyes.

- Take your right hand, place it on your throat and use your left hand to place it on your heart. Focus on these two organs as you breathe in and out in a relaxed manner. Feel the muscles on your neck and chest relax entirely with your touch.

- Place both your hands beneath your chest across from each other. The top of the middle fingers should be touching. Focus on the energy from your hands and to that area, and allow the muscles in your chest and ribs to relax as you breathe.

- Hold the previous hand position and move a bit further down over your upper stomach. Concentrate on relaxing your muscles in that area. Remember to breathe in deeply and slowly.

- Keep the same position and move toward the lower part of your stomach on your belly button. Maintain your breathing and feel the energy flowing across this part while relaxing your abdominal muscles.

- Touch your shoulder by folding your arms backward with your elbows in front of you. Focus your attention on the muscles in this area. Most people carry tension in the neck and shoulders, so take this moment to relax this area while breathing deeply in and out.

- Touch the area below your waist where your kidneys are located with your hands on the opposite sides. Feel the relaxation seeping in your muscles and maintain your breathing.

- Place your hands on your feet. You can fold your legs in any position that feels comfortable so that you can easily reach your feet. Hold this position while breathing and focus on relaxing your muscles in the soles of your feet.

You can try other meditations, like a guided meditation involving an instructor pacing you through the steps to perform. This type of meditation works if you have trouble focusing on your breathing or are easily distracted. You can also listen to meditation videos and perform the steps as instructed. Don't be discouraged if one type of meditation didn't work. We encourage you to try more than one method to determine which feels the most natural. This way, you will have a better chance of sustaining this practice daily, which is the key to opening your mind to access your Akashic Records.

Past Life Regression Meditation

This type of meditation is usually performed under the guidance of a professional therapist. The therapist begins the session with specific instructions to help you relax. Once you are in a relaxed state, the therapist proceeds by encouraging you to remember past memories of events you experienced in your past lives. The whole concept of this therapy is to help you discover specific details about yourself. It helps you learn more about particular behaviors wired into you without understanding the reasons behind them.

When you learn about the emotions you carry from your past lives, you will better understand what triggers you. The goal is to let go of any trauma or negativity you hold from another life. Sometimes, you may find a connection with your higher self or a higher power and receive messages or directions that will guide you through your life.

With some practice, you can perform this meditation therapy by yourself. However, it is not recommended unless you have spent a long time performing it under a therapist's guidance. You may encounter upsetting memories that are too overwhelming and cause trauma in your current life.

When you want to access your past life, a starting point would be to look at familiar places, people, talents, food, or anything you feel is natural to you. You can also find some hints in your dreams, but it takes a lot of skill to remember them. Sometimes, we have dreams that seem too real. These dreams could be a clue you are picking up from a past life. When you go into a meditative state, think about your desired outcomes. Tell yourself that you want information about your past. This is what set intention means when attempting to access your Akashic Records. Practice asking for information before going to bed or performing a meditative practice. You may receive random memories when you do this practice, and these memories can help you learn valuable information about your past lives.

Symptoms of an Unclear Mind

Your mind may be filled with constant noise and clutter that hinders your ability to focus on your meditation or relax. An unclear mind makes you anxious, stressed, and unable to focus on regular tasks. This state can also be termed as brain fog, where you feel mentally drained all the time. You may feel numb and unable to feel excited or happy about doing any activity. It may take you an hour to perform a task that used to take minutes. These feelings contribute to your inability to focus since you are easily distracted.

All the symptoms are derived from each other. When your brain is foggy or hazy, you feel distracted and anxious. Your anxiety fills your mind with negative thoughts, and all of your energy goes toward eliminating these thoughts. Easy assignments might seem gruesome to you because you don't have the headspace to perform any task, no matter how simple.

Even when you are doing a simple task like performing a chore at home, your head may be filled with anxious thoughts. This is how anxiety leads to more anxiety and brain fog. Take the following test to find out if you relate to these symptoms. If most of your answers are "Agree" and "Strongly Agree," you probably have an unclear mind.

1. I usually worry about a lot of different things.
- Strongly Agree
- Agree
- Neither Agree nor Disagree
- Disagree
- Strongly Disagree

2. I have trouble controlling my negative thoughts.

- Strongly Agree
- Agree
- Neither Agree nor Disagree
- Disagree
- Strongly Disagree

3. I feel easily agitated when I am stressed.

- Strongly Agree
- Agree
- Neither Agree nor Disagree
- Disagree
- Strongly Disagree

4. I worry my stress is making me feel exhausted.

- Strongly Agree
- Agree
- Neither Agree nor Disagree
- Disagree
- Strongly Disagree

5. I worry that my anxiety contributes to my lack of focus.

- Strongly Agree
- Agree
- Neither Agree nor Disagree
- Disagree
- Strongly Disagree

6. I worry that my anxiety hinders my ability to sleep well.

- Strongly Agree
- Agree

- Neither Agree nor Disagree
- Disagree
- Strongly Disagree

7. I always feel nervous.

- Strongly Agree
- Agree
- Neither Agree nor Disagree
- Disagree
- Strongly Disagree

8. I always worry that I am not doing a good job.

- Strongly Agree
- Agree
- Neither Agree nor Disagree
- Disagree
- Strongly Disagree

9. I worry about the future a lot.

- Strongly Agree
- Agree
- Neither Agree nor Disagree
- Disagree
- Strongly Disagree

10. I worry about events that happened in the past.

- Strongly Agree
- Agree
- Neither Agree nor Disagree
- Disagree

- Strongly Disagree

11. My muscles usually tense up when I feel nervous or stressed.

- Strongly Agree
- Agree
- Neither Agree nor Disagree
- Disagree
- Strongly Disagree

This chapter discussed a few meditative exercises you can try at home. We mentioned some symptoms you may experience with an unclear mind. We encourage you to try different methods to find one that suits you the best. Finding a mindful mental exercise you like will help you continue practicing cleansing your mind of any negative energy.

Chapter 8: Cleansing Your Space

The space you use to meditate in has to be free from negative energy. You can't focus on breathing exercises and meditation when your space has clogged energy. A quiet, relaxing room with good energy flow will help you clear your mind so that you are open to receiving information through your Akashic Records. This chapter discusses a few methods you can use to cleanse your meditative space.

Smudging

This cleansing method helps to clear any negative energy present in your house. It involves burning a plant to produce smoke responsible for purifying the surrounding air from any negativity. Many types of plant material can be used for cleansing and purifying your environment. Palo santo is one of the most commonly used wooden materials in smudging. It is indigenous to South America and produces a zesty, bright, and sweet smell that brightens up a room instantly, making it the go-to material in daily smudging.

A popular herb used for cleansing is white sage and is widely used in stuffy rooms with clogged energy because of its strong presence. White sage is a perfect choice if you want to cleanse your whole house. White sage produces a heavy cleanse as it provides a healing environment by purifying the negative energy. When burned, white sage has a sweet and woodsy scent.

Some herbs promote a relaxing environment due to their essential oils content. These include aspen, which is used for protection by blocking bad energy. The essential oils help reduce anxiety, providing the optimum environment for meditation. Bay leaves also contain essential oils and are usually used for protection and healing.

Lemongrass has a refreshing scent used as an energy booster as it helps promote a clean environment where you can focus better during meditation. Cinnamon also helps boost energy and improve your mood as it allows good fortune and promotes motivation and healing. Rosemary has a soothing effect and helps provide a peaceful environment. Cedar is usually added to a sage bundle because it burns for a long time and is commonly used for protection against negative energy.

Eucalyptus is used in smudging for health benefits and is perfect for cleansing your meditative space. Lavender promotes a relaxing atmosphere at night to help you sleep better. It is typically combined with blue sage or desert sage in a bundle. Desert sage helps drive away negative emotions. Pine is commonly used for cleansing and protection, and it promotes good health and fortune. Catnip promotes happiness and joy in a living space and is perfect for a cleansing ritual like smudging. Cloves produce a sweet, fragrant scent that carries dark energy away from your space.

Other plant material used in smudging can include chamomile, ginger, thyme, basil, lilac, amaranth, myrrh, allspice, frankincense, and mugwort, among others. White sage is usually made into a bundle with a few herbs attached and burned to promote protection and cleansing. Many of these herbs are also used in incense cleansing and discussed later in this chapter.

When you perform smudging, make sure you take your time. You have to be mindful of choosing your herbs and where to place them, so don't rush into the process. Remind yourself to breathe and focus on your breathing rhythm to help you slow down. Organize the herbs on your altar and make sure they are only used for cleansing and protection purposes.

Prepare a candle on the altar, light it with a match, and use the lit candle to light your herb bundle. It's better to use a fire-resistant container to avoid any accidents from the burning herbs. Some people use abalone shells as a container for falling ash, and the abalone shell serves as the water element in this ritual. Make sure the container is only used for cleansing purposes. Another important element in this ritual is having a clay pot filled with sand. After you finish smudging, use the sand to extinguish the burning bundle.

If you still feel a bit tense before the smudging ritual, take a step back and relax. Perform a short meditation session by doing a simple breathing exercise. If you are performing the ritual with other people, ask them to join using other methods like sound or incense. Set your intention before the ritual to speak what your heart desires. Say what you wish for yourself and your loved ones.

When you cleanse your space from negative energy, you want your set intentions to occupy the cleansed space. Once you have everything prepared, you can start the smudging ritual.

Move from the front door of your house to the rest of the house, taking each area one by one while holding the burning herb bundle. Walk slowly, moving clockwise around the house. Allow the smoke to pass through every corner in the house and even closed areas like the attic, garage, basement, and closets. This type of movement has been performed over the ages, and it is how many old cultures cleansed their homes and sacred spaces. Recite a prayer or chant a mantra to increase spiritual vibrations in your house.

You should end up where you started at the front door when you've been through the whole house. Recite a final prayer, look at your newly cleared house, and imagine it filled with brightness. Finally, say your wishes and intentions one more time before you end the ritual.

Incense Cleansing

Many cultures use incense to clear negative energy from their homes. Some people use incense to protect their new business space, car, or other objects to avoid being affected with bad energy and misfortune. Incense cleansing involves burning plant material like smudging, but dried plants and resins are also used. Incense is made from natural materials considered sacred. These include frankincense, sandalwood, and many others listed later. These plants are considered sacred because they transfer energetic vibrations to your space. When you burn incense in your home, the smoke purifies it and spreads positivity and peace. They are used for protection purposes by blocking negative energy that has lower vibrations from your home.

Similar to smudging, white sage and other herbs are also used in incense cleansing. You can combine resin with herbs with this method to produce a much more powerful effect. Also, use incense sticks that serve the same purpose. Palo santo and aloeswood are wooden incense commonly used in cleansing. There are a few popular options with incense, each having specific properties.

Copal resin is excellent for promoting good energy flow. It helps remove clogged energy in your house and is believed to open the crown chakra. Myrrh is used in incense cleansing as a mood booster as it promotes positivity by increasing energetic vibrations. It is always a good idea to incorporate myrrh with any incense burning as it aids in amplifying their effect.

Benzoin works wonders when used as incense as it elevates the mood and opens the heart chakra. It is always recommended to use it during emotional moments like going through a breakup or losing a loved one. Frankincense is used to cleanse your space and protect it from negative vibes. It helps open your mind to receive information from your subconscious mind about your past lives, making it a perfect choice for cleansing and meditative purposes.

Palo santo can be used as-is or in its resin form to allow positivity back in your house. Its name translates to "holy wood," which is why it is considered a sacred plant material and is usually used during meditation. Styrax is used in incense cleansing for protection, and it explicitly promotes a positive influence on your finances. Set your intentions to call for wealth and abundance while burning this incense in your house or business.

Now, let's move on to stick incense. All the herbs mentioned in smudging can be used as incense. Sandalwood promotes strength and power and is mostly used to boost confidence and uplift your spirits when you feel down. A similar incense is amber, which boosts your self-esteem because it is connected to your solar plexus chakra.

Nag champa has similar effects as white sage and is commonly used by yoga practitioners as it carries high vibrations that promote cleansing and purifying vibes. It also helps increase the collective vibrations in your house. Lotus opens the crown chakra like copal resin and also helps get you in touch with your higher self. It is perfect for meditation as it promotes a peaceful, calming environment. Lavender has a calming effect and promotes relaxation, and reduces anxiety. Patchouli also helps bring calmness to your mind, helping to put you in a meditative state. It is the perfect incense to burn if you have an unclear mind.

When performing incense cleansing or smudging, you are encouraged to recite prayers, chant mantras, or just speak your intentions aloud. If all you want is to clear your space of negative energy, simply say, *"I invite energetic vibrations in my house and expel negative vibes away from my house."* You can say affirmative statements like *"I am calm, and all my worries are melting away."* Say whatever feels natural to you, but be clear about what you want. It is essential to take your time in the whole cleansing process because you must be mindful of what you say and do during cleansing rituals.

There is no specific time to cleanse your home. Just do it whenever you feel there is stagnant energy in your house. You can perform a cleansing ritual whenever you have people over, especially if you feel their presence brought negative vibes to your house. You may want to cleanse your house when you are recovering from major surgery, illness, or emotional distress. Cleansing your home in these cases is like a clean slate you are giving your mind, body, and soul.

Each cleansing session depends on the size of your house or the area you want to cleanse. If you feel the smoke is too much and is burning your senses, then it's time to cut it short. If you feel there are still areas that need cleaning in your house, then continue the ritual for a while longer until you feel the whole house is cleared of negative energy.

An important tip to bear in mind when burning incense or smudging is to allow the smoke to take the negative energy away from the house. You can't perform the ritual in a closed space. Open all your windows to allow bad energy to exit so that you can replace it with positive energy. It is also advisable to perform a self-smudging ritual bypassing the burning bundle or incense around your body. You can do this even before cleansing your home for better results.

Sound Cleansing

Sound greatly impacts our lives, especially the spirit. Different sounds trigger various effects that we first perceive emotionally, and they resonate in the body. Listening to gentle sounds helps you to feel calmer and more relaxed, so play soft music to help get your mind off things. It is no secret that gentle sounds have a specific frequency that promotes calming and cleansing, which clears your space from bad energy.

Since ancient times, sound has been used in various rituals and meditative practices to bring peace and harmony to a space or community. Different tools created specific sounds, like bells and crystal bowls. Crystal bowls or singing bowls are arranged in a set, with each bowl tuned to a certain note. They are played together as an instrument to compose a harmonious melody that promotes calming vibrations. This experience is referred to as sound baths because it represents an intrinsic bath to your spirit. You feel that any bad feelings you have are washed away listening to the lovely sounds of musical instruments.

There are musical notes specific to cleansing. If you learn how to perform this type of cleansing, it will significantly impact the process of space cleansing at your home. Sound cleansing is even more powerful than smudging and incense cleansing – and effectively clears out the toughest energy blocks, where the other methods fail.

A few tools can be used in sound cleansing. Singing bowls are among the most powerful tools in this type of cleansing because it helps to blast through stagnant energy. Metallic bowls are most effective in cleansing rituals. A mallet creates a sound by hitting the sides or circling it around the rim of the bowl. The latter technique produces a lasting sound. You can create your own melody as you move throughout your house and let the sound resonate in your space. Direct the sound to move upward, downward, and across every area in your house.

A bell is a popular choice in sound cleansing, as you can simply ring a bell in your meditation space to bring positive energy to the room. The sound vibrations help break up clogged energy and boost the energy left in the room. Use drums to cleanse your space as they are perfect for breaking up stagnant energy. Simply beat the drum in a rhythmic pattern while walking clockwise around the house.

Chanting helps to rejuvenate energy in the house and your spirit. You can use chants to drive away negative energy and restore balance in the house. Also, use clapping as a rhythm when you chant. Clapping is a cleansing technique, especially if you don't have other tools. The easiest thing to do is use your voice and hands to drive away negative energy from your house and meditative space. Chant and clap as you walk clockwise around the house and make sure the sounds you produce reach every corner in your house.

This chapter discussed a few methods used to cleanse your space. These practices promote protection against negative energy and help the process of healing from any previous trauma. Cleansing your space helps reduce your anxiety and allows you to focus on your meditation sessions, which is the ultimate way to access your Akashic Records.

Chapter 9: Connecting to Your Spirit Guides

Spirit guides all are around us; they send us messages, guide, and protect us. When you are about to make a decision, and you hear a voice telling you "don't do this" or "this is a bad idea," you believe this voice to be your gut feeling or a voice in your head. However, this inner voice is your spirit guide talking to you and helping you. Spirit guides are, as it is clear from the name, guides, and helpers in the form of evolved spiritual beings who help, teach, heal, and protect you as you navigate life. In other words, spirit guides are very similar to the concept of guardian angels.

The physical realm where we exist isn't the only one. There are many other realms out there, including the higher realm. As human beings, we are entirely unaware of what goes on in the higher realm where spirits and other beings exist. Spirit guides communicate with us in the physical realm to offer us the assistance and guidance we need. A spirit guide was once a regular spirit living on our Earth but has finished its journey and incarnation. They have learned many lessons through the many lives they lived in our realm, so they have unmatched wisdom and a higher perspective to offer us advice and enlightenment once we connect with them.

Connecting with your spiritual guide requires you to strengthen your sixth sense because a heightened sixth sense makes you more aware of the spiritual world. We all have spirit guides who never leave our side and are there for us from the day we are born until we die. There is something so comforting about the idea that we aren't alone and have assistance in life's more significant decisions. A spirit guide can make your life better, and it's nice to know we aren't going through this journey alone. Your spirit guide is always there, reaching out to you, sending you signs, and nudging you to make the right decisions.

Our spirit guides reach out to us in various ways. They want to help us and are always trying to reach out. Figuring out their methods of communication enables you to receive their messages and benefit from their guidance. Your spirit guide may send you a message through a dream, connect while you meditate, speak to you using your intuition or gut feeling, or send you clear signs. There is no such thing as a coincidence, so if you struggle with a decision and dream or see a sign in the street regarding this decision, then pay attention. Your spirit guide is trying to tell you something. Sometimes you may also feel the urge to do something or act in a particular way, but you don't really understand why - this is your spirit guide nudging you in the right direction.

You have definitely been contacted by your spirit guide and benefited from their assistance or protection before, even if you aren't aware of it. Although your spirit guide is always there and willing to help, communicating with them doesn't come easy for everyone. However, becoming more spiritual enables you to connect with your spirit guide. Even if you think it is too much work, it is worth it to have a relationship with your spirit guide. They have lived for hundreds or thousands of years and lived many different lives. Additionally, they have also been with you since the day you were born, so they know you more than anyone else, making them better equipped to give you advice. To benefit from the wisdom and guidance of your spirit guide, you must figure out how to connect with them.

How to Connect with Your Spirit Guide

Set the Mood

You need to create a sacred space to connect with your spirit guide. It is a very important step that you shouldn't skip, especially if it is your first time reaching out to a spirit guide. We live in a fast-paced world full of many distractions and noise. To shut out the external world and focus inward, you need to be mindful of the here and now. Focusing inward will allow you to reach the higher realm where your spirit guide exists so you can communicate with them. You can set the mood by sitting in a quiet and comfortable spot, lighting a candle, and dimming the lights. Using crystals can also help set the mood.

Clear Your Thoughts

Clearing your thoughts is a critical step toward connecting with your spirit guides. You need to clear your thoughts and only focus on contacting your spirit guide and what you want to ask them. This step will make it easy to conjure up the right spirit guides for the decisions you are struggling with.

Practice Relaxation Methods

After setting the mood and clearing your mind, comes relaxation. Your body and mind need to be relaxed, and you should only focus on your breath. Don't overthink what you are doing or worry about what it will feel like once you establish a connection with your spirit guide. It is hard to anticipate how or what this experience will feel like, especially your first time. It may be a strong connection or a very subtle one. However, in time your connection will deepen and become stronger. For now, limit your expectations, let go, and enjoy the experience.

Feel Your Energy

Relaxation allows you to be centered and to feel the energy from every part of your body. You need to feel everything around you; and that you are one with the earth and light. Let the light go through you till it reaches your root chakra and every part of you. Open yourself up to the light and energy surrounding you and let them lift you.

Chant

To raise your vibrations and harmonize your energy with the spirits, you should try chanting. Chanting the "om" sound a few times will match with the divine and open a portal.

Walk through the Portal

Now, you will start to feel something different deep down. It is your body's light turning on to attract your spirit's guide. Stay focused on this light since it represents your pure spirit. Picture yourself going through a portal taking you to a different dimension. This "portal" will look different for each person; some will see it as a door, while others will see a landscape. After walking through the portal, you will feel the universe expanding around you, which means you are ready to connect with your spirit guide. Call on them and invite them to join you. If you don't give your spirit guide explicit permission to join you, they will not communicate with you. Your permission is a must.

Receive the Message

You and your spirit guide are now connected, and they are ready to send you messages to guide you. However, you shouldn't expect these messages to be clear or black or white. The message can come in the form of a smell, vision, feeling, or a thought. For this reason, you need to be extremely focused and attuned to your feelings because you can receive messages in many unexpected ways.

Request a Sign or a Message

Naturally, you want to feel reassured of your connection with your spirit guide. So, make it a habit to ask them for signs to confirm that they are with you and reaffirm your faith in them. If you ask in a loving, gentle manner, they will happily oblige. Besides reassurance, take advantage of your connection with them and ask them to send you messages to guide you or advise you with whatever decisions you are struggling with. Remember, your spirit guide is always willing to help, and sometimes all you have to do is ask.

Come Back

Once you receive your message or sign, you need to return to the physical realm. It is crucial that you come back the same way you went through the portal. If you struggle with your return, ask your spirit guide to show you the way. As you take your journey back, you need to make sure you don't leave any pieces of your soul behind. Take your time to return to your body entirely.

This could mean different things to different people. Some prefer to sit in silence and focus on their breathing as they take it all in. Some focus on their energy and the shift they've experienced. Meanwhile, others prefer to practice the child's pose, also known by its Sanskrit name, Balasana, which is considered a restorative pose with calming properties.

After every encounter, you will feel different as a result of achieving a connection with the spirit world. Do normal everyday things like eating or taking a walk so that you can go back to your usual self.

Make it a habit to visit and connect with your spirit guide every day. Don't only go to them when you need their guidance but also show your gratitude and strengthen your relationship with them. Communicating with your spirit guide is important if you want to gain access to your Akashic Records. Your spirit guides will train you to trust your sight, hearing, and feelings. When you access your Akashic Records and ask a question, your spirit guide will be the one helping you to read your records and uncover your truth. They will give you answers by speaking to you, sending you images, making you sense, or instinctively *knowing* certain things. If you have trouble interpreting these messages, your spirit guide will walk you through them.

As we have mentioned, there are different spirit guides. To strengthen your relationship with your spirit guide, you need to understand what types of spirits you are trying to connect with. Since each person may have more than one spirit guide, it is safe to say various spirits are guiding you.

Types of Spirit Guides

Angels

There are three types of angels; guardian angels, archangels, and helper angels. Do you know how some people usually say your guardian angel saved you? It turns out that this isn't just a metaphor. Spirit guides come in the form of guardian angels, and you have more than one guardian angel helping and guiding you. Anytime you need assistance, seek your guardian angel's help. Regardless of your faith or religion, guardian angels don't discriminate and are willing to help everyone as they love all people equally. Each person is assigned a guardian angel from birth.

In the world of angels, archangels are considered leaders with a very powerful presence and energy. When an empath connects to an archangel, they immediately feel that the energy in the room has altered. There are different archangels, and each one has a name and specialty. For instance, Rafael, the Healer, can help heal your body, mind, and spirit. There is also an archangel called Gabriel the Messenger, whose specialty is to send you clear messages.

The last type of angel is the helper angel. Their job is to find humans who need help and offer assistance in certain situations, like helping you make new friends or find a new job.

Spirit Animals

Spirit guides also come in the form of a spirit animal. There are as many types of spirit animals as there are animals, each with a lesson to teach. For instance, if you have problems with your self-esteem, a peacock will be your spirit animal to guide you to be more confident. A spirit animal can also be a deceased pet who becomes your spirit guide. Your spirit animal will first appear to you in a dream or at your home in your backyard.

Ascended Masters

An ascended master was once a human being who lived in our world and led a spiritual life like Mother Mary or Buddha. Now that their journey in the physical world is over, they serve as leaders in the spiritual world to guide and teach us. All ascended masters work together as a unit despite their religion or faith when they once roamed the physical world.

Deceased Loved Ones

It is always a comforting thought when someone tells us that our dearly departed are never truly gone. The more you read and learn about spirit guides, the more you will discover that this is true. Although the people who loved us and passed on are no longer with us, their love still remains. A family member or a friend who passed away may still want to be there for you and guide you by choosing to be your spirit guide. They can show their love, support, protection, and guidance in an authentic way from heaven. For instance, they can save you from a bad relationship or help you strengthen good ones. Even family members we didn't know who passed away can choose to help and guide us.

In addition to your loved ones, any deceased person can be your spirit guide if they feel you can benefit from their wisdom. For instance, if you are a doctor or want to be, your spirit guide could have been a doctor when they were alive to guide and inspire you on your journey.

Our Ancestors

Our connection to our ancestors runs deeply. While we are all connected in more ways than one, ancestral bonds can be a special type of connection. They can be our fierce protectors willing to provide us with guidance and wisdom. For this reason, when establishing communication with your spirit guides, connect to your ancestors first. They will help show you the way, and in many cases, they can be the ones bringing you the message you need to hear.

Keep your eyes, ears, soul, and mind open. Spirit guides are all around us, sending signs and messages. You just need to recognize them to receive these messages. However, living a hectic life full of distractions makes these messages more obscure. So, always keep your eyes and mind open to receive them. Be mindful of the moment you are living in, as this awareness makes it easy to notice the signs surrounding you and listen to the voices trying to speak to you. Always be on the lookout for signs, especially when you need them the most. For instance, you have been offered a job in another state and are contemplating whether to move or not. You need to keep your eyes open as your spirit guides nudge you toward the right decision. For instance, if the job is in New York, you may be given a book about New York or hear a friend telling you how great living in New York is. You may even get a clear message seeing an ad that says, "Come to New York." There are messages and signs everywhere around you. Your spirit guides are always trying to communicate with you, so don't brush something off as imagination or coincidence. Listen to your gut feeling or that little voice in your head. If you are struggling with a decision and have seen a sign in the street or a friend says something you find helpful, don't ignore them. It is your spirit guide communicating with you. You aren't alone in this journey. You are guided and supported, so open your senses and surrender yourself to your spirit guides.

Chapter 10: Identify Your Intentions

If you ask Google how you can access Akashic Records, you will come across hundreds of thousands of results. Most of them will comprise practitioners on YouTube and hypnosis programs claiming to help viewers access Akashic Records or transcend into the extraterrestrial hallowed halls.

Individuals able to access these records may come in contact with angels, guides, and other forces working behind the scenes. Many people explain that accessing the Akashic Records is one means of channeling, though others report that they pretty much just receive information through their dreams.

As soon as people understand the Akashic Records, many expect to scroll through their lives when accessing these records. However, from what those who have accessed the records have explained, it seems like each individual experiences something different. Temple-like conditions, images of guides, audible instructions, or messages, and even a screening of one's past life are among the experiences people have reported. It means that each likely individual sees, hears, or feels something unique and significant to them.

The whole point behind Akashic Records and reading is getting to the main source. It allows you to identify the core issue you're struggling with or where all your troubles began. This is necessary to ensure that you heal as deeply and as profoundly as you should. There are multiple layers of belief, integration, fear, and perception. Your experience highly depends on your capacity to face specific fears or come in contact with your limitations.

While many people can access the Akashic Records on their first try, others may have to keep trying for weeks or even months on end before finally succeeding. Therefore, it's always best to approach your attempts with no expectations whatsoever. According to practitioners, staying persistent, dedicated, and viewing your failure as a recurring lesson can bring about great results in the end. Just like each person's experience varies, there isn't a single set way you can access the records. Upon reading various blog posts, articles, and books, talking to many practitioners, or watching several YouTube videos, you'll come to realize that countless methods are allowing you access to the Akashic Records. Although, you still need to know that many of these techniques carry similar fundamental principles.

Regardless of the method you decide to use, you always need to be clear about what you want to know. Perhaps you are looking for a specific piece of information, or maybe you're just exploring or browsing. No matter what your motive is, you need to have defined, clear-cut intentions, such as "I want to learn about my past-life," "I want to verify the Akashic Records' existence," or "I want to explore the realm of the records." Think of any questions you want to ask or specific answers you're seeking. Identifying and setting your intentions are key to your success at accessing the realm, and this is why you need to spend as much time as the process takes. Writing down your thoughts can be a great help. Not receiving an answer doesn't mean you set wrong intentions or asked the wrong questions. There is no right or wrong way when accessing the records. It just happens that you may ask something and not get an answer in return. When you're ready, it's then time to dive right in. Even if you don't know them, ask your guides to guide you in this journey.

This chapter will discuss why it's so important to identify precisely what you want to get out of accessing the Akashic Records. If you're still unsure, reading this chapter can aid you in identifying your intentions and also learning how to set your intention based on your reasoning.

The Importance of Intention

To understand the importance of intention for accessing the Akashic Records, you must realize the power behind intention in general. We find it very hard to attach a specific meaning to the word "intention." Intention can mean many things and apply to numerous cases and scenarios. However, if we must define it, then "being committed to acquiring something or acting a certain way" would be a great interpretation of the word.

Let's say you're worried that something may not go in the direction you thought it would. For instance, if you're on your way to buy the shirt you saw and immediately fell in love with while window shopping, you may worry that it's already sold out. However, when you're working with intentions, the flow of events differs slightly. Setting an intention means that you're preparing yourself to have and act. Being prepared is almost synonymous with being certain that something will occur. In other words, why would you prepare yourself for something you know isn't going to happen? Believing in your intention can help you garner the results you want because it influences your subconscious, aligning it with your intention's frequency, even if your intention is working with your guides or angels. You need to realize that the true power lies within your subconscious, which is fueled by your intention.

When accessing the records, you should always aim for quality instead of hoping for accuracy because energies shift considerably, making it impossible to nail every detail down. If you want a quality experience, you (and anyone helping you) must have pure intentions and be present. You must have an open mind and an open heart. It means that you must have courage, discernment, trust, humility, and be happy to discover new things. The general environment and your inner state must be calm and peaceful.

The intention is a fundamental aspect of any type of energy work, especially Akashic Record readings, because the reading or experience is fueled by the questions and intentions of the individual. If you want quality, you must always begin with intention.

Attempting to explore the records without intentions leaves your guides on hold. While you don't want to do this, having pure intentions is much better than just being clear about them. So, if you're visiting a reader or practitioner, you must make sure that their flow and interpretations will not be clouded by their opinions, judgment, and preconceptions. Setting your intention helps you realize whether you're genuinely ready to delve deep into your problems and accomplish profound healing.

This, of course, doesn't mean opting out when things don't go according to plan. Setting an intention isn't like planning an itinerary. It is a state of mind. It must be done with acceptance of the fact that, sometimes, your journey may lead you where you need to go instead of where you want to go or where you hoped to go. This, in particular, tends to apply to people who only feel safe when they are in control of their environment. If this happens, turn your focus to what is rather than what "should have been," and trust the journey, and more importantly, yourself.

Setting Your Intentions

Setting your intention is not an easy thing to do, especially if you're not sure about your current position in life, what you would like to let go of the direction you're headed, and where you'd like to be. In this case, it's easier to direct your focus toward a specific direction or a particular problem or obstacle.

It requires you to do some inner searching and reflection. Is there something that you'd like to learn about yourself? What is it? Think about where you mainly learn your strongest and greatest lessons. Have you noticed a pattern in the situations, people, places, or problems that teach you these lessons? Reflect on the aspects you can benefit from opening yourself more fully? How can you do it? Finally, you must think about everything you must and want to let go of.

Once you have solid answers, you can then set your intentions. Use statements like "I want to release...," "I want to do/incorporate...," "I want to learn...," and "I want my future step to be...." Every few days or each week, take a look at your answers, your intention statements, what you have achieved so far, and where you're going. Our intentions are constantly changing, meaning that you can benefit from repeating this process as many times as you want to help you to identify and set your intentions consciously.

How to Intend

As you may recall, the intention is the opposite of worry and hesitation. It is about getting your energy to align instantly with the things you desire. So, how can you do it?

The questions mentioned above can help you get a clearer picture of what you want to find out. Not knowing what to search for may grant you information that isn't in your best interest. For instance, your true purpose can be achieving internal balance, yet you ask how you can attract a partner into your life.

You also need to keep yourself aligned with the information you're seeking. You can do that by understanding how Akashic Records work and having faith that you will acquire all the answers. You need to truly believe that all you seek will come to pass with every bit of your being. Keep in mind that you shouldn't rely on transcending to the realm of the record to receive these answers, meaning that you should keep an eye on physical sources of information, like videos, books, and images.

Finally, you have to be accepting, open, and receptive. Setting your intention requires you to be positive and sure that the answers and information you seek are already yours. You need to let go and wait for the universe or higher powers to offer you the answers. You must be receptive in return because you will probably only receive answers through your intuition unless you're very experienced with Akashic Records or have psychic abilities. Don't seek your answers consciously because they will always come whenever you least expect them. Your answers will arise from your subconscious, or appear through a physical resource, as we mentioned when you're participating in even the most mundane activities. You don't need to search for information actively. Instead, all you need to do is keep an open eye, an open heart, and stay receptive. If you need to exert the effort to find the answer you're searching for, this is something that your intuition will also let you know. Either way, the more educated you are on a subject, the more likely you'll pick up on the signs or relate to new information on the issue. If you're not knowledgeable enough about the subject, how will you be able to identify the signs?

It can be challenging to determine whether you're genuinely committed to your intention. Commitment is vital because it allows you to receive more specific guidance on your journey. You need to realize whether your intentions are just wishful and hopeful or decision-based. If they're full of nothing but hope, you will never get precise and proper guidance.

It helps to remember that you are responsible for creating and shaping your own experience. Many people expect their intuition and guides to take the reins, forgetting that their will is the driving force in life, even with the spiritual resources they lean into for help. Before seeking guidance, you need to ask yourself about the extent to which you are committed to your intentions. You need to determine if you're ready to take steps forward, possibly change various aspects of your life, and get out of your comfort zone. These are all aspects that will help you manifest the life you want.

Some people are more "committed" to intentions that come easily. They are only dedicated if they don't have to spend plenty of time and effort or change anything in their lives. Countless people struggle to receive clear guidance and information, thinking they haven't yet connected with their intuition. What they don't realize is that the main problem is their own commitment level.

Setting your intentions is a vital facet of accessing Akashic Records. It is fundamental to various energy healing methods and techniques. It's not easy to identify your intentions, especially when you're unaware of your current position in life and where you'd like to be. However, by finding out the things you want to discover, aligning yourself with the information you're searching for, and being open, accepting, and receptive, you will be able to set your intentions successfully.

Chapter 11: The Prayer Method

Now that you have familiarized yourself with the concept of the Akashic Records and learned how to prepare your mind and body for receiving their wisdom, it's time for you to delve into the practical side of forging your pathway to Akasha. This chapter discusses the most popular method of opening the Records, and that is through prayer. Having an opening and closing prayer is a crucial part of this process, and an example for each is provided herewith. You will also learn about the benefits of using this method and modifying it to fit your beliefs and purposes.

The Benefits of the Prayer Method

As you have surmised from the previous chapter, opening the Akashic Records will require you to be in a relaxed state with your mind focused on your intention. It's all about shifting your conscious state of awareness into a place where you become open to receiving information from a higher dimension. This shift should be subtle and not forced or urged in any way. The prayer method is a simple yet effective way to facilitate this shift. Furthermore, your success in accessing information relating to yourself depends on your ability to trust your intuition. Using your instincts as guidance towards reaching Akasha requires a unique approach that comes from a state of self-love. In addition, when preparing for a session, you must ensure your emotions are balanced. One of the biggest obstacles you may encounter during this process is dealing with a cluster of negative emotions. You may have a sense of urgency to find the answer to a pressing question or be desperate to learn more about yourself, or you may even be dreading what you will uncover in your records. Unfortunately, by hesitating in your mind during your session, these doubtful emotions may limit your ability to retrieve the answers you are looking for. Therefore, giving in to them will be counterproductive for your purpose because if you let your negative thoughts and feelings prevail, you cannot focus on expressing love through your intent. Reciting a prayer to open your Akashic Records will help you frame your mind to receive the proper loving guidance from your inner self.

If you aren't familiar with prayers or typically use them, you will probably find this process challenging. Depending on your belief system, you may be conditioned to look at prayers as a way to ask for something, whether seeking help from a deity, a spiritual leader or any other entity - it's typically a force outside yourself. However, doing this will instill a codependent mindset, one you depend on and leading you toward the desired outcome. It is problematic because it doesn't let you explore your own power. After all, if you keep asking the records for help, how will you know what you are capable of? To successfully open your Akashic Records, you must look at prayer as a manifestation of your intention. Using your voice to bring your desires to life is a much more productive way to use prayer. Focusing your mind on your instinctual desires gives you the power to collect all your ideas and manifest them according to your wishes. Through this, you become the co-creator of your destiny - something that opening and reading your Akashic Records will definitely require you to be.

On the other hand, if you have heard of prayers being used by psychics in an unfamiliar way, you may think of this as a form of fortune-telling. However, the Akashic Record should only be for guidance when you aren't sure which direction to take in life. The wisdom you revive from them works best if you are inspired to receive it. What better way to create a motivating atmosphere than tapping into your spiritual beliefs with a prayer? Connecting to spirituality can mean different things to each one of us. You may think of it as expressing love, seeing goodness in you and others, igniting the power that lies within your soul, or becoming one with a deity of your choice. Whichever direction your belief system takes you, it only matters that you discover the energy that allows you to connect to Akasha and open your Records.

A great thing about the Akashic Records is that you don't need a psychic or reader to open them, and you don't need to become one either. Each of us has the ability to become aware of our thoughts, actions, emotions, and soul. With a prayer, discovering the wisdom of all universes and your connection with them is only a step away. So, if you are ready to empower yourself with spiritual awareness through Akasha and transform your life, feel free to use the prayers below.

Prayers for Opening and Closing the Akashic Records

Before beginning the prayer, you must enter a cohesive state of mind through your preferred relaxation method. It's a good idea to do this when you are alone to not be disturbed during the process. Allow yourself at least 30 minutes of peace and quiet for your first session. As your spirituality advances, you will be able to fine-tune your questions more and more, allowing you to gain the answers in 10-15 minutes at the most.

It's also recommended to prepare the questions you want to ask the Records beforehand. Opening the Records can be a confusing experience, and you may even forget what you are looking for. If this happens, you won't retrieve the wisdom you need, and all the good work you did focusing on your intent during prayer will go to waste. Write your questions on a piece of paper so that you can read them when you have opened the records. It's recommended to begin with one or two questions for your first session, and by cultivating your wisdom, you can slowly expand your list. The intent will become much more transparent, with practice allowing you to omit writing down your questions and form them when preparing for prayer.

You should also prepare a pen and a blank piece of paper - you will need these to write down the answers you receive. The more information you get in one session, the easier it will be to access the

Records the next time. Writing down all you hear, see, or feel during the process helps avoid forgetting an essential piece of information and missing out on a chance of learning more about yourself.

When you feel ready, take a deep breath, and start drawing in as much energy as possible through your thoughts and self-will to manifest your higher self. You may choose to close your eyes if you feel it helps you concentrate, but if you feel more comfortable keeping them open, feel free to do so. You can also place your hand on your body as a reminder to focus on your inner self. If you are working with a deity or spirit, now is the time to invite them. You may now recite the following opening prayer out loud:

> *I hereby acknowledge the forces of the Universe and its spirits*
>
> *I ask them for direction, guidance and to learn the truth*
>
> *I wish to know what I can do*
>
> *So, I can be protected from my ego*
>
> *As it is to be revealed in the form of the higher good*
>
> *I come from a place of love and compassion*
>
> *While I stay connected to everything around me*
>
> *Recordkeepers helped me learn everything about (your name) from the Akashic Records.*
>
> *So, I can see (your name) through the access of my guides, my loved ones, past and present.*
>
> *And share the wisdom and compassion I now gain with everyone deserving.*
>
> *From this moment onward, anything I hear, see and feel is a message intended for (your name).*
>
> *My Akashic Records are now open.*

Repeat the entire prayer two more times silently to ensure your intent resonates clearly. When you reach Akasha, you may feel a little uncomfortable at first. Leave yourself some time until you can sense positive energy surrounding you. Describe what you see, hear, or feel to yourself. This will help you remember to channel it the next time when opening your records through prayer. Move on to ask the questions you previously prepared. Wait until you receive the response, and be prepared to receive it in whatever form it comes in. Once you feel you have gained enough inspiration, guidance, or answers to all your questions, you may proceed with closing the records. To do this, you will need to recite the following closing prayer.

I am thankful for ancestral spirits, my guides, and the universe for the wisdom they have bestowed upon me today.

I am also grateful for the help of Recordkeepers in allowing me to open my records and access their information.

I promise to use this knowledge solely for the purpose of a higher good.

My Akashic Records are now closed.

Repeat this prayer twice more in your mind as you did with the opening prayer.

Make sure you utilize your current legal name in the prayers when using this method for the first time. It will help the Recordkeepers to locate your information. Once you have familiarized yourself with Akasha, you may substitute your name for the word myself.

The first part of the opening prayer is about creating a sacred space by tapping into your spirituality. After manifesting your intent, this is the second most important part of the prayer. You will be opening yourself up to all forms of energy, some of them coming from different universes. Creating a sacred place will help you define the type of energy you come in contact with during your session. You can also set the perimeters of how you wish to engage with this source of universal wisdom.

The second part is for further clarifying what your intentions are. This is where you determine what you want to achieve and how. If you have any specific requirements for receiving the information, you may define it now. For example, you can choose how long the message will last. The more information you request, the longer it will take for the Recordkeepers to translate it.

The third part refers to where you are coming from. As with all methods of spiritual exploration, the best place to start your journey is within yourself. By yourself, it's understood that you will be using your heart and not your mind. Spirituality comes from emotions, not from your thoughts, so it stands to reason to rely on your heart. Tap into the love, compassion, and all your other positive feelings when reciting this part.

Lastly, you mention who will deliver the message to you. The Recordkeepers have a tremendous role in retrieving and translating the information you are seeking. Honoring these beings in your prayer will encourage them to work for you more efficiently.

The closing prayer has the purpose of restoring your consciousness to your normal state. It serves as a transitional period helping your mind and body adjust to mundane emotions and thoughts instead of the elevated ones you experience in the enlightened state. During this time, most memory loss occurs about what happened throughout your session. To avoid this, you will want to be extra careful. Taking a couple of deep breaths usually helps you calmly get through this adjustment period.

While this may seem like a short prayer, it's this length for a reason. It's designed to help beginners focus on their intent by narrowing down the choices. Naturally, if you want to include another intention, you are free to do so. For example, if you find it hard to interpret the messages, you may ask for a specific message you can validate. This may be a specific color, sound, or feeling you recognize and relate to. As long as it serves as a suitable filter for understanding the universal wisdom, you can use it in your prayer. However, in the beginning, the messages may be confusing regardless of the medium you are receiving them through.

Another crucial part of successful prayer is acknowledging that everything you will perceive during your session is part of the message you are meant to receive. Remember, the wisdom from the Akashic Records can reach you in many forms. Its energy can enter your body or any object around you. So, everything that happens during the session should be accepted as if it is coming from the Records. You may be tempted to question the sounds you hear or the physical symptoms you feel, but this will only distract you from your goal. For this reason, you must accept everything as part of the process without any doubt and hesitation.

This prayer method is a tool for opening your Akashic Records and gathering ancient wisdom and an excellent way to explore your spirituality, find your inner peace, and experience love and compassion. Even being guided through it the first time using these prayers, you can establish a profound spiritual connection with your inner self. This alone could be worth giving the method a chance. When you add the impact exploring the Records can have on your life, you could have everything you desire and deserve. No, it won't provide you with magical results, but its most significant benefit lies precisely in that. If you want results, you will have to dedicate time and attention to achieving them.

Additional Tips for Using the Prayer Method

If you are merely delving into this method, you will undoubtedly benefit from the ones provided in this chapter. Even if you aren't yet ready to open your Records, you can still benefit from the energy contained in these prayers. In contrast, if you merely tried to create a pathway on your own, the process of reaching the gates of Akasha would take much longer. Prayer works so well for opening the Akashic Records because the spoken intention is an energy field emanating from a person's body. So, every time someone creates a prayer, their energy is transferred to this tool and, eventually, to whoever uses it. Initially, this will make it easier to familiarize yourself with spiritual energy. Working with it will help you see the difference it can bring to your life, including elevating your spirituality.

Be mindful of everything you notice at any moment while you access the Records. All the sensations are the manifestation of energy coming from Akasha, like the words of your prayer. Don't be discouraged if you aren't successful the first time you try your luck with this method. In fact, during the first few tries, you may not notice anything different at all, and this is entirely normal, especially if you are just beginning to explore your spirituality. Learning to use prayers for opening the Akashic Records takes time and practice. As you become more familiar with expressing a loving, honest intention, you will be able to access your Records. Ultimately, you might find it far easier than you thought it to be in the beginning.

Over time, you may even learn to create your own prayer, which will empower your journey to Akasha even more. Many spiritual seekers feel the urge to form their own pathway. This enlightenment is usually a result of receiving parts of the universal wisdom from the Akashic Records. If this happens to you, you will be ready to start modifying prayers to suit your needs. When doing this, think about each word you use as a tool for your intent. Every word has its purpose, energy, and impact on the Akashic Records. The more personal they are, the more compelling their effect on helping you gain the answers you are desiring. Using this newfound knowledge and spiritual energy, you will be able to achieve more formidable results.

Chapter 12: The Meditation Method

Now that you have learned about the Akashic Records and how to access them through prayer, we will discuss another popular method: meditation. As already mentioned, anyone can access and read their Akashic Records once they learn the correct way. Before going any further, we must stress that there is no right or wrong way to access your Akashic Records. You can try various methods until you find the one that works for you.

Meditation

Meditation is another method that can help you access your Akashic Records. To connect to your spirit guide, you must first clear your mind. You will need to connect with your spirit guide so that they can help you access your records. Meditation allows you to clear your thoughts and be mindful to shut out the external world and direct your focus inward.

As you probably know, the Akashic Records exist in a higher plane. So, to access them, you will need to alter your vibrational frequency to match the higher plane's frequency. The best way to adjust your frequency is through meditation. However, the meditation process doesn't need to be a long one. Meditating for a long time will make you feel fatigued and unable to concentrate. Losing focus will make it hard for you to access your Akashic Records. Therefore, stick to 15 minutes or less for meditation. Hydration is an essential part of meditation. Before you start, drink a glass or two of water. Your brain and body must be hydrated to get the best out of your reading experience. Additionally, you shouldn't try to access your Akashic Records on a full stomach, as you may feel sick in the middle of the process. So, if you are hungry, eat a small, light meal before you start.

The higher realm isn't always safe because many dangerous entities exist there. Another advantage to meditation is that it creates a shield to guard you and protect you from getting attacked by these dangerous entities.

Meditation will help get you to this state of mind by keeping you relaxed, calming your brain, and helping you reach inner peace.

How to Meditate to Access Akashic Records

The first step is to find a quiet and comfortable place far away from any distractions. Sit in a comfortable spot, close your eyes, and breathe slowly while focusing on your breath. These steps are similar to regular meditation most people do daily to either calm themselves down or be mindful. The following steps will help you access your Akashic Records. You need to clear your mind and set your intentions on the questions you want to be answered. Start by saying a prayer. It doesn't have to be a specific prayer, just speak from the heart and pray that you will remember this experience and all of the information and knowledge you will gather. Finish your prayer with gratitude.

Keep your eyes closed and ask for the divine light to surround you. As mentioned, spirit guides play a huge role in helping you access your records. Therefore, during your meditation process, call on your spirit guide or guardian angel, along with the Archangel Metatron. Ask them to help you access your Akashic Records so that you can gain knowledge, truth, wisdom, and healing from any past events or traumatic experiences. Remain calm, relaxed, and keep focused on your breathing for some time. To feel more relaxed and eliminate tension, imagine yourself inhaling love, strength, and positive energy while exhaling all the negative emotions, stress, and pain. You are breathing in light and letting go of all the darkness consuming you. Keep doing this for a while as you focus inward. It is important to raise your frequency and vibration to reach the Akashic Records. When you feel you have reached this higher level, call on the Archangel Metatron and request his guidance to help you reach the Akashic Record dimensional understanding. You need to feel that you are being lifted. You can do this by imagining getting into an elevator made of light that takes you to a higher level. You are rising towards the light, and you are one with the spirit, source, and all that is.

Open your heart, expand your mind, and let love, light, and positive energy wash over you while you are lifted by the elevator of light. You are now one with all the divine connections and sources. With your guardian angel by your side, keep going higher. Now, the elevator will stop, and you will step out and into a sacred place. You have arrived at your destination in the realm of the Akashic Records. Naturally, you want to read your records and fulfill your goals. However, take this moment just to be and simply exist. Afterward, allow yourself to feel all the knowledge floating around you. You are in the presence of something great, and you are surrounded by not only your records but also every being that has ever existed records' too. We are all connected. Can you feel it? Feel how every action each person takes affects you and everyone else. Every choice you and everyone make has an echo that is heard by all other beings because we are all connected. Every action we take has a ripple effect. You are connected to these actions even if they aren't yours. You are connected to people, things, the universe, and the records.

Once you feel this connection, it is time to access your records. You can do this by merely thinking of something you need guidance with or a question that you want to be answered. Metatron will, in turn, guide you towards the answers you are seeking by helping you access your records. You won't get answers the same way you do in the physical world. Answers in this realm will appear differently. You may feel that the Archangel Metatron is giving you a book, or you see a mental image or a movie, hear a voice or feel something. You may even find yourself consumed with all of the knowledge and information you need in this stage of your life. Each person will receive their answers differently, so remain focused and aware to find what you are looking for.

Remember, you aren't alone in this process. You are guided by your guardian angel and Metatron. During this process, you may fall victim to feelings of doubt. Although these feelings are normal, you shouldn't give in to them or let them disturb your peace. However, we are humans, and these feelings are natural. So, if you feel any doubt or feel your thoughts have wandered, ask the Archangel Michael for help to calm your thoughts so that you can stay focused. Now, get ready to receive your answers. Open your heart and mind to grasp all the information the Akashic Records are providing you with.

After receiving the answers or information, it is time to go back to the physical realm. However, before leaving, you must thank the Akasha records and all the angels who helped you. They need to feel that you appreciate what they did for you. Return the same way, using the elevator of light. Once you feel you are back in the physical realm, write down your experience. You need to write down everything you have seen, felt, or heard because the answers you seek lie in them. However, if you can't remember everything, that's ok. Take your time and relax, and it will come to you eventually. If you feel the answers are confusing or unclear, ask your spirit guide to help make things clear.

Don't expect to figure everything out or have a full understanding of the whole process from a single visit. Keep practicing, and you will gather more information with each visit and benefit from the wisdom of the Akashic Records. If this is your first time practicing meditation to access your records, consider doing a guided meditation first to help you reach the required mental state. The more you practice, the less you will need guided meditation, and you will reach this state yourself.

Practice Mindful Meditation

You need to practice mindful meditation regularly to effortlessly reach the state of mind that will help you access the Akashic Records. Mindful meditation takes a few minutes and benefits your mind and well-being since it keeps you focused on the moment and increases your awareness.

Find a Quiet Spot

As mentioned earlier, you need to find a quiet spot with no distractions so you can be entirely focused. You should get comfortable by either sitting on a chair, the floor, or a cushion. You can also lie down if this will make you more comfortable. If you are seated, make sure that you sit up straight but not so that it makes you stiff. Place your arms and legs where you feel most comfortable.

Feel Your Body

Be aware of your body and notice what it is feeling at this very moment while you are seated or lying down. Experience every sensation in every part of your body, like what your hands or legs are touching and your body's connection with the chair or floor. Make sure you are relaxed completely and allow your body to release any tension.

Focus on Your Breath

Breathing is the gateway to meditation. We breathe every day to stay alive, and we are never aware of the process or focus on it. So, you need to feel the air getting in and out of your lungs. Breathe naturally like you always do, but be mindful of the inhaling and exhaling process.

One technique that can help you breathe mindfully is by putting the same simple intention into every breath. As we said, breathing is what we do to stay alive. In other words, when we allow ourselves to breathe, we give ourselves the gift of life. Every breath we breathe is an act of love. Focusing on the core intention behind your breathing will help ease you into the process.

Stay Focused

Remain focused on your breathing and shut out the world around you. Only focus on the here and now. However, you may feel that your mind starts to wander at times. We live very fast-paced and hectic lives. Our minds are always racing, so they are never used to slowing down or relaxing a bit. You may find the external world creeping in by thinking about different things like work, family, or the bills you have to pay. While this can be frustrating, it is very normal, so don't be harsh on yourself. Since you are practicing mindfulness, it will be easy to notice when your mind wanders. When this happens, all you need to do is shift your attention back to the "here and now" or current moment and focus on your breathing.

If you are still facing difficulty clearing your mind, here's a helpful technique to aid you. Picture yourself standing on the side of the road. As your thoughts start to flow, picture them as passing cars. Often, we are tempted to get in one of those cars by engaging our thoughts. Don't. Simply hold your ground and observe the cars as they pass by. The less you engage with your thoughts, the quieter your mind will be. Before you know it, the road will be completely empty, and your mind will become still as a lake.

You may find yourself relying on this technique in the beginning. Then, as with training wheels, you'll naturally grow less reliant on the visualization.

Keep Breathing

Keep breathing and focusing on your breath for about five to ten minutes. Every time your mind wanders, bring it back. Ensure that you are entirely relaxed.

You can keep your eyes opened or closed, whatever makes you comfortable. However, if you practice meditation to access the Akashic Records, your eyes must be closed. It enables you to go on your journey and receive any visual messages or signs. Practice mindful breathing meditation every day. It is highly beneficial for your mental health since it lowers stress and anxiety and keeps you focused on the present moment, so you won't obsess over the future or worry about the past.

Being mindful allows you to be aware of the world around you. You need to be aware and focused to notice all the signs and messages your spiritual guide is sending you. When you are mindful, all your senses will focus on the here and now, so you will be attuned to what the universe tells you. The universe is always speaking to us. All we need to do is listen and open our hearts.

Chapter 13: The Visualization Method

This chapter discusses the visualization method. This method is a skill that can help you access your Akashic Records and find out information about yourself and others to make better life decisions. To practice this skill, we've listed a few exercises throughout the chapter so that you can improve your skills. At the end of the chapter, step-by-step instructions on how to do this method are included, so you don't have any trouble.

What Is Visualization?

Visualization is the ability to see images in your mind. These images can be anything you want them to be, and they often come as a surprise. When you can visualize, you tap into your subconscious mind, which contains all the information you have ever seen or experienced in your life. It also includes information about other people.

Akashic Records Are the Library of the Soul

As discussed in the previous chapters, Akashic Records are an infinite library containing all knowledge. They exist within your body and mind and externally around you (in other people). These are records of our past, present, and future. You can access this information by becoming calm enough to hear and learn from it. However, there is a lot of noise in our everyday lives preventing us from hearing this information. This is where visualization comes into play.

Visualization and Akashic Records

The visualization method is a powerful way to access information from the Akashic Records. The Akashic Records are a spiritual database containing all information about every person and event in history.

The visualization method involves picturing yourself in a sacred space, such as a temple or your personal sanctuary. In this space, you can ask any question you want about your life, and the Akashic Records will provide you with an answer.

Visually picture yourself in a temple or another sacred space (the key here is to make it as real as possible). Imagine two doors before you; one door leads into darkness, and the other leads into the light. Visualize walking through the door into the light.

Once inside the temple, visualize a staircase that leads down below ground level (you can picture yourself descending this staircase, or you can allow your mind to take you to another place). Once underground, imagine entering an expansive room with wall-to-wall bookshelves. This is the Akashic Records library, where all information about your life and the lives of others is stored.

Now, ask any question you want about your life, and the Akashic Records will answer. The answers may come as thoughts, images, or feelings. Trust that the information you receive is accurate and relevant to your current situation.

The visualization method is a powerful way to access information from the Akashic Records.

How to Practice Visualization

The visualization method is one of the most important techniques for practicing meditation. It is a way to see and experience the world as it truly is, without any filters or judgments.

To practice visualization, sit in a comfortable position and close your eyes. Take a few deep breaths and let go of all thoughts and distractions. When you are ready, visualize yourself in a place that brings you peace and happiness. It could be a beautiful garden, a mountaintop, or anywhere else that feels calming and peaceful.

See the sights and sounds around you in elaborate detail. Feel the sun on your skin or the wind blowing through your hair. Take in the smells of the flowers or the fresh air. Listen to the birds singing or the wind blowing through the trees.

Keep in mind that it's your place. You are allowed to fill it with anything and everything you want. Perhaps you've always connected with a particular plant or have felt comfort around the presence of a certain animal. Feel free to bring them in. The goal is not only to practice visualization but also to create a safe space that serves as your center point.

When you are finished, thank the place for bringing you peace and happiness. Slowly open your eyes and begin your day.

Learning to Visualize takes practice. It may be helpful to practice visualization for a few minutes every day until you become skilled at it. The more you practice, the easier it will be to access information from the Akashic Records.

Frequency of Practice

The more you practice visualization, the easier it will become to access information from the Akashic Records.

Visualization should ideally take place every day for at least a few minutes. You can also visualize during other activities, like when you are walking around town or doing your daily chores and tasks. Just make sure that you spend a little time visualizing yourself in a sacred space each day.

By practicing visualization every day, you will begin to see the world as it truly is and gain access to information from the Akashic Records to guide you on your life path.

The more often you practice visualization, the easier it becomes for your mind to connect with higher realms of consciousness and receive information from the Akashic Records. Try to visualize every day for at least a few minutes, and you will notice an improvement in your ability to connect with this spiritual database.

Simple Visualization Techniques for Beginners

Visualization is a very powerful tool for gaining knowledge and insight. It can also be instrumental in helping you to see the world as it truly is, rather than how we think or judge it to be.

People use many variations of visualization, such as guided imagery, meditation, active imagination, daydreaming, lucid dreaming, guided meditation, and many more. Of course, not everyone will want or need to use all of these methods, but it helps to know about them so that you have the option should you choose to try them out in the future.

Guided Imagery

Guided imagery is a visualization that is led or suggested by another person. This person can be a therapist, a teacher, or a friend. They will typically guide you through a visualization exercise using verbal instructions and images.

Meditation

Meditation is the practice of quieting the mind and focusing on one thing, such as your breath or a mantra. Most people meditate for a specific period (like five minutes) and repeat this process several times.

Active Imagination

An active imagination is similar to guided imagery but is done alone without any verbal guidance or images. You simply sit quietly by yourself and create mental pictures in the Akashic Records library.

Daydreaming

Daydreaming is a visualization that we all experience from time to time. It is merely letting the mind wander without any specific focus or goal.

Lucid Dreaming

Lucid dreaming is the ability to be aware that you are dreaming and control the dream. It can be done by simply asking a dream character or knowing that you are dreaming.

It is best to regularly practice and use many different visualizations to gain the most from visualization. It allows you to learn more about your mind and receive valuable information from your subconscious thoughts and feelings.

Mental Visualization Exercise #1

The first mental visualization exercise is to imagine your favorite place. It can be anywhere in the world or even a made-up place. The most important thing is that it's a place where you feel happy and at peace.

Close your eyes and take a few deep breaths. Once you're relaxed, picture yourself standing in your favorite place. See the sights and sounds around you, feel the sun or wind on your skin, and smell the air. Stay here for a few minutes, taking it all in.

When you're ready, slowly return to reality. Take a few more deep breaths and open your eyes. Write down how this exercise made you feel.

You could write something like this:

The visualization exercise made me feel happy and at peace. It was a nice break from reality, and it was fun to imagine myself in my favorite place. I felt like I could truly relax and take it all in. It was a nice mental break.

Mental Visualization Exercise #2

The second mental visualization exercise is to imagine a situation that made you feel happy or joyful. It could be something from your past or something you're looking forward to in the future.

Close your eyes and take a few deep breaths. Once you're relaxed, picture yourself in this happy situation. See the sights and sounds around you, feel the happiness and joy in your heart, and smell the air. Stay here for a few minutes, taking it all in.

When you're ready, slowly return to reality. Take a few more deep breaths and open your eyes. Write down how this exercise made you feel.

You could write something like this:

The visualization exercise made me feel happy and joyful. It was a nice break from reality, and it was fun to imagine myself in my favorite situation. I felt like I could truly relax and take it all in. It was a nice mental break.

Mental Visualization Exercise #3

The third mental visualization exercise is to imagine yourself achieving your goal. See yourself achieving your goal in great detail, and feel the happiness and satisfaction that comes with it.

Close your eyes and take a few deep breaths. Once you're relaxed, picture yourself achieving your goal. See the sights and sounds around you, feel the happiness and satisfaction in your heart, and smell the air. Stay here for a few minutes, taking it all in.

When you're ready, slowly return to reality. Take a few more deep breaths and open your eyes. Write down how this exercise made you feel.

You could write something like this:

The visualization exercise made me feel happy and at peace because achieving my goal would be an incredible feeling I look forward to. It was a nice break from reality, and it was fun to imagine myself in my favorite situation. I felt like I could truly relax and take it all in. It was a nice mental break.

Mental Visualization Exercise #4

The next mental visualization exercise is to imagine yourself as you want to be. See yourself as you want to be in great detail, and feel the happiness and satisfaction that comes with it.

Close your eyes and take a few deep breaths. Once you're relaxed, picture yourself as you want to be. See the sights and sounds around you, feel the happiness and satisfaction in your heart, and smell the air. Stay here for a few minutes, taking it all in.

When you're ready, slowly return to reality. Take a few more deep breaths and open your eyes. Write down how this exercise made you feel.

You could write something like this:

The visualization exercise made me feel happy and peaceful because being true to myself makes me happy and fulfilled. It was a nice break from reality, and it was fun to imagine myself in my favorite situation. I felt like I could truly relax and take it all in. It was a nice mental break.

Mental Visualization Exercise #5

The fifth mental visualization exercise is to imagine yourself being kind and compassionate towards others. See yourself being kind and compassionate towards others in great detail, and feel the happiness and satisfaction that comes with it.

Close your eyes and take a few deep breaths. Once you're relaxed, picture yourself being kind and compassionate towards others. See the sights and sounds around you, feel the happiness and satisfaction in your heart, and smell the air. Stay here for a few minutes, taking it all in.

When you're ready, slowly return to reality. Take a few more deep breaths and open your eyes. Write down how this exercise made you feel.

You could write something like this:

The visualization exercise made me feel happy and fulfilled because being kind makes everyone around me feel good and appreciated. It was a nice break from reality, and it was fun to imagine myself in my favorite situation. I felt like I could truly relax and take it all in. It was a nice mental break.

Mental Visualization Exercise #6

The last visualization exercise is to imagine your child self in your happy place. Observe their body language, what they are doing and how they are feeling. Then, when you are ready, introduce your current self to the place and to your child self.

Here are some questions to help guide your interaction:

- How would the introduction go? What's the first thing that you would do?
- What would your child self want to say to you? And what would you want to say to them?
- What would they think of you? What would you think of them?
- In the end, ask permission to hug your child self.

You may be tempted to orchestrate the interaction, but try to resist. Participate, listen, and let the interaction unfold. As healing as it can be, such an interaction can also be heavy in nature. Before you leap to your notebook and journal about it, take the time to breathe and slowly return to your body.

Accessing Akashic Records via Visualization

Another way to access the Akashic Records is through visualization. This powerful act of imagination allows you to see your life objectively. It's like looking at yourself from the outside, without biases and fears getting in the way.

Step-by-Step Guide to Visualize Akashic Records

The following is a step-by-step guide on how to visualize the Akashic Records:

Step: 1

Close your eyes and take a few deep breaths.

Step: 2

Once you're relaxed, picture yourself walking through an old library with thousands of records lining the shelves. It's very dimly lit except for small lamps on each shelf casting shadows around you. The smell of dust fills the air as you walk past row after row of these record books. There's a feeling of power and knowledge in the air.

Step: 3

As you walk down the aisle, you will find the book that corresponds to your life. It's marked with your name and birthdate. You take it off the shelf and open it to see your entire life story written inside.

Step: 4

See yourself walking through each moment of your life and see the decisions you made and the consequences that followed. See yourself as you are now and how your decisions have led you to this point.

Step: 5

When you've finished, close the book, and return it to its place on the shelf. Walk back out of the library and slowly return to reality.

Document Your Experience

You could write something like this:

> *I visualized myself walking through an old library with thousands of records lining the shelves. I walked down the aisle and found my record, marked with my name and birthdate. It was opened to seeing my entire life story written inside so that I could go back in time and review each moment.*
>
> *The experience was very powerful, and it allowed me to see my life objectively without all my biases and fears getting in the way. I could understand how my decisions have led*

me to this point, and it gave me a lot of insight into the future. It was an amazing experience that I'll never forget.

Beginner Guidance for Accessing Akashic Records

If you're just starting your spiritual journey and wish to access the Akashic Records, there are a few things you should know. First of all, it's important not to get too caught up in what they refer to as "past lives" because we don't have past lives. They only exist through our memories.

Instead, focus on the present and how you can use the knowledge from the Akashic Records to improve your present life. You may also want to start by working on your personal development before accessing the records of others. It will help you build the strong foundation necessary for correctly accessing the records.

There are many ways to access these records, but visualization is one of the easiest and most effective methods for beginners. It's also an excellent way to practice accessing them before moving on to more advanced techniques to understand better past lives or people with whom you may have had karmic connections in your current life.

The Akashic Records is one of the most powerful tools for accessing knowledge you can find. It's up to you whether or not this method will work for you, but it certainly has helped many people in their spiritual journeys. Once you have tried it for yourself, you can better judge its potential uses.

The visualization method is merely one way to access the Akashic Records. If this particular approach doesn't work for you, don't give up, there are plenty of other more suitable techniques. The most important thing is to keep exploring and learning as much as possible about this fascinating topic.

Chapter 14: Accessing Others' Records

If your experience with opening the Akashic Records has inspired you to share their benefits with others, feel free to do so. After all, as mentioned previously, anyone who is spiritually enlightened and has the ability to raise their vibration can access the Records. Not only can they access their Records, but anything that has energy because, if they have energy, they also have stored memory. If you want to access information about anyone, you only need to gain access to a higher energy plane. You may do this through your preferred method, and it's only a question of training. However, a few rules apply when accessing someone else's Akashic Records. This chapter helps you explore these rules, along with the steps it takes to become a successful conveyor of messages received from the Akashic plane.

The Challenges of Accessing Others' Records

The Akashic Records represent an infinite source of information connected to an energetic field. When you own Records, your energy serves as a medium for harnessing the knowledge you seek. However, your soul must be ready to accept wisdom and grow through its help. It makes communicating with the Akashic field very personal, but your own energy levels only limit you. When you try to gather information for another person, you will have far less energy to rely on. You only have access to the emotions and energetic state they show you through their inquiry about the process and their explanation of what they want to achieve. Since this doesn't give you an insight into their soul, you may not be able to provide them with the exact guidance they need. You may receive and relay some of the messages meant for them but miss others because you aren't in tune with the energy that connects these records. Raising your vibrations helps you access more information about them despite not vibrating on the same frequency. For this to work, you must practice extensively and ensure you follow all of the rules of the Akashic plane.

The Process of Accessing Others' Records

Despite all the challenges, the basis of the process of accessing someone else's Akashic Records is pretty much the same as for you. You will need to follow the same steps, beginning with getting yourself in a relaxed state of mind. The only exception is that you need to include the other person in the process. Whether you choose to open the Records through meditation, prayer, or any other way, it should help ground both of you. During the process of opening their Records, you will need to state that you are representing the person and you have their permission. When you feel connected with their Records, make sure to verify this by checking their content against their personal information. Typically, you will receive an opening statement regarding the Records' owner. It's advisable to relay this to them immediately so they can be sure you are indeed accessing their Records. After this confirmation, proceed with asking the questions they seek answers for. Whether it's uncovering negative patterns, healing, or guidance they need, you need to emphasize this during your inquiry. It allows the person to receive knowledge to help them resolve all emotional and energetic issues and move forward with their life healthier. Once you feel you have received and relayed all the wisdom the person needs at that moment, you may close the Records.

Again, you can do this using your usual method. However, you may want to do this slower than you would for yourself. They may need more time to transition back to reality and process the information they have received, particularly if the message was upsetting. In addition, people who aren't used to receiving spiritual messages will usually have questions after the session. Answer their questions regarding the messages to the best of your ability, or if you can't, suggest to them other means for getting their answers. The entire process, from the time you begin relaxing to when the person receives all the clarification they need, may last double the time than it would for accessing your Records. This is entirely normal, and you must make sure the other person understands they can take all the time they need.

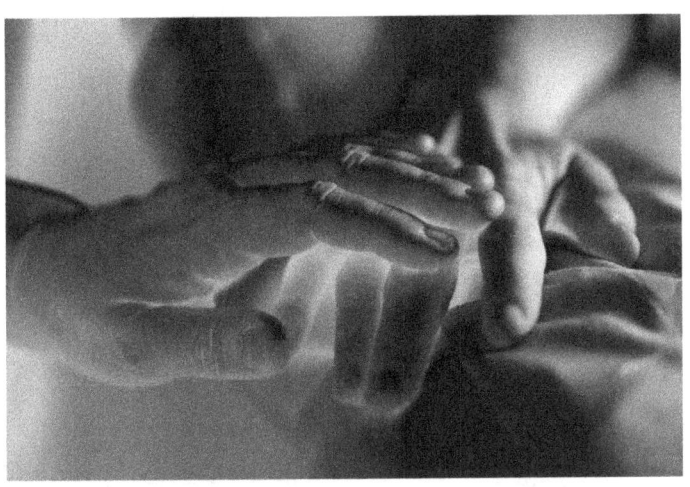

It Starts with You

One of the crucial factors determining whether you can open someone else's Records is your approach to the session. First and foremost, you will need to be clear about why you seek access to their information. You must have a clear intention of relaying the knowledge meant for someone else, meaning if you are just curious about someone else's actions, past, or future, it doesn't give you the right to look into their Records, not even when you feel that their future could be connected to yours, or if you know the person well and you only mean to help them. Going behind their back is never advisable, and it also won't allow you to open the records. The connection between a person's vibrating energetic field and their Akashic Records also serves as a spiritual shield against prying eyes. It ensures the information that belongs only to them is kept hidden until they are ready to retrieve it. Furthermore, accessing something out of curiosity and without their knowledge lowers vibrations. Since this leads to an ego-driven state of mind, you will emit negative energy blocked by the gate to the Akashic Records, which is another way to protect them.

The best way to approach the opening of the Akashic Records for others is with honorable intentions. There is nothing wrong with wanting to help someone, but you may only suggest gaining them access to the guidance they need. Whether they take up on your offer for reading their Records is up to them. Moreover, the intention for accessing a person's universal knowledge has to be benevolent. Looking into your colleague's experiences isn't a valid reason either, even if you are in competition with them and curious about their actions. When accessing someone's information, you can only do it if it's in their best interest. In whatever form or time it comes, the message has to contribute to their life positively.

Due to all the reasons mentioned above, the only authentic way to receive messages meant for others is to gain their consent. This permission has to come from their soul, and they must be willing to accept any message, answer, guidance, or resolution they receive.

Practice Is Important

The saying "practice makes perfect" never rang truer than when you learn how to access someone else's spiritual information. In the beginning, you may be unsure of whether you are led by your energy or *their* energy. The best way to practice avoiding mistaking your information for theirs - and getting the full effect - is to do this is with people you don't know. Asking for their current legal name and date of birth will ensure you access the appropriate records. The more precisely you pinpoint one's experiences, the clearer the limiting patterns, past trauma, or any other obstacle will be. It will help them overcome obstacles and transform their lives as it did yours. Whether the experience they face now (or their ancestors faced), it can help them find peace, understanding, wisdom, and hope.

When gathering all this, you must keep your soul's desires at bay. The problem is if you have a close relationship with the person, your wishful thoughts for helping them can cloud your judgment while retrieving their Akashic messages. Influencing your mind to conjure the outcome you desire is not wise, even when accessing your Records. Your assumptions can be even worse for the people you know well. This is another way practicing with strangers can come in handy. When someone asks you to read their Records, they may be tempted to provide an in-depth explanation of their reasons for doing so. Encourage them only to provide you with the question they want to be answered, name, date of birth, and nothing more. Or, if they feel the need to explain their challenges, they should only do this before the session begins. By not knowing anything about their issue in advance, you can avoid forming assumptions that stand in the way of a successful reading. Once you practice this enough times, you will be able to separate your energy from the other person's energy, allowing you to concentrate only on their Records.

Apart from this, you will also be free to gather more information from the person in question. It opens the possibility for discussing their goals, recurring themes, and difficulties, which may help them form the appropriate question. For example, they may feel stuck in their current life and would like to know if taking a particular step would get them closer to moving past this stage of their life. You may explain to them that the best course of action isn't asking whether something happens in the future or not. A better solution would be to check their progress as they work towards their goal. It's also a good idea for pregnant women to avoid looking into their unborn child's Records. After all, the child has its soul, meaning the information belongs to them, only they aren't able to voice their opinion yet.

Additional Tips for Accessing Others' Records

Always clarify how the Akashic Records communicate with you and the person whose information you are about to unlock. All their past actions and traumas form a particular energetic imprint within the Records. However, different imprints are typically translated to different messages. To properly convey the messages to their owner, you must absorb and interpret them correctly. Practicing with your Akashic Records helps you learn which messages you are more likely to interpret correctly.

By now, you are probably getting only the knowledge you can use. With other people, the messages can be different from those you are accustomed to getting, particularly if the person's vibrational energy differs vastly from your own. One or two of your senses is typically heightened for receiving wisdom for yourself. However, you must be prepared for the knowledge others will receive to come from any of your senses. By correctly interpreting the message, you can help the person identify the issue's root. For example, if you rely on your vision, you may see a scene that's related to the feeling of guilt. You will only identify it as guilt if you know how the Akashic Records typically present the messages to you. This will also facilitate conveying the message verbally, which is another challenge you might face. When receiving information meant for you, you may find it easy to align it with your soul and feel what they mean. Explaining them to others may be a lot more challenging, even more so, if the person isn't familiar with spiritual exploration. Moreover, coming up with a suitable solution for their issue is only possible if they can understand where their issues are coming from. Encourage them to embrace the message and look at it as an opportunity to improve their life. It may be scary to confront a mistake from the past or present, but they must understand they have nothing to be ashamed of. Maintaining a calm voice helps reassure them that it's worth facing whatever challenge they must endure to find the best solution.

Another issue you may face is getting the person you are working with to agree to share their past experiences. They may be ashamed of their past actions or simply don't feel they are relevant to their current situation. In any event, you must recognize when someone isn't entirely open to let you see everything that's stored in their records. Their openness determines their vibrational energy, which affects yours, too. Therefore, it's a prerequisite for a successful reading. Make sure you press on the importance of this topic during consultation before you proceed to open the gates of wisdom. To receive the knowledge they need, they must fully open themselves to the experience. Otherwise, the information you get is either negative or distorted and will not be helpful at all.

Despite your best efforts to suppress them, your emotions might still affect the process of accessing others' records. Being under a lot of stress may render you unable to focus on the person's energy and provide them with the desired results. If you experience anything unusual during the reading and suspect it has to do with your negative emotions, you must stop the session. Explain to the person that you cannot access their Records currently, and you need to clear your head before continuing. They will appreciate your openness and be happy to return for reading when it's more convenient for both of you.

Ultimately, you must remember to create a safe space for the person whose Records you are accessing. People interested in gaining access to their information are often in a vulnerable state of mind. They either feel stuck in a loop or want to know why things are going wrong in their life. Even if you are accessing the Records of someone close to you, they will rely on your help to find a way to heal or guide them along their path. While retrieving the universal wisdom may help them see the reasons behind their current and past actions, it only works if you connect to their soul and energetic field. A person dealing with insecurities needs resolution, and if you cannot provide them with it, it makes things worse. Without it, they cannot move on with their life. Your inability to provide them with their Records will only add to their distress. In addition, if the concept of vibrations and energy levels is foreign to them, they may feel highly intimidated by the prospect of an Akashic reading. Making them feel welcomed and loved, you honor them, which, in itself, has an uplifting effect on their soul. It will also put them at ease, so they will be more receptive to the messages you retrieve on their behalf. As they get comfortable, their vibrations will rise, facilitating the opening of their Records.

While reading for someone who seeks to understand past traumas is about them, not you, but the information you access can also benefit you. Showing respect for the people whose life experiences differ from yours also helps you grow as a person. When you start reading the Akashic Records of others, you may bypass information you don't understand. By learning about the grievances of their soul, or their ancestors' souls, you develop a much deeper sense of compassion. It opens up the possibility for a path of enlightenment and self-development from which you and others can equally benefit. This allows you to become more open to their messages, learn to interpret them better, and help more people along the line. You will also learn to recognize when your energy isn't high enough to help someone heal. You will realize that referring them to someone who has more experience in the area they need assistance in helps them much more. It may take many years of personal and spiritual development to get to this point. But, when you do, it will all be worth it. When you reach this stage, you will step into a much higher energy plane, and you will take pride in everything you do for yourself, your loved ones, and the world.

Chapter 15: Akashic Records FAQs

Many people have questions about Akashic Records. It's understandable to be curious and want to know more before making a decision that might change your life. Therefore, we've compiled this FAQ for those interested in learning more about what the records can do and how they work so you can make an informed decision.

What are the Akashic Records?

The Akashic Records are a place where all your thoughts, words, and deeds go. They are a record of your past, present, and future. The records consist of every thought you've ever had in your life. When we access these records, what is being accessed is not just our personal records but also those of other people linked to us through various connections, such as family members, friends, co-workers, or even experiences we may have shared with them. The best part is that we all have the power to benefit from the information within the records. Just by connecting to the subtle elements of nature and existence, we can answer all the questions that puzzle us.

What do I need to see my records?

To access the records, you need a clear intention and be in a calm and relaxed state. You don't necessarily need to go into a trance or deep meditation, but it is helpful if you can quiet your mind and focus on your request. It also helps if your chakras are aligned since the enhanced energy flow, and elevated vibrations help you achieve a higher level of connection to the subtle parts of existence, such as the Akashic Records.

Can I ask specific questions about my life?

Yes! It is best to ask specific questions to get the most accurate results. If you're not sure what information you should be looking for, we recommend asking these two main questions:

What events and experiences were significant (or traumatic) in my life? What choices did I make or things that happened influenced the course of my life?

Keep in mind that while some answers may not be direct and tailored to you, they are still highly accurate. Due to the objective nature of the records, answers often come in the shape of concepts that we may not have arrived at with our current thinking process.

What do I need to know right now to help me move forward in my life? How long does it take for the records to respond?

The answer to this question depends on a few factors. How clear your request is and how easily you connect with the records. In some cases, people receive their answers within a few moments. In contrast, those new to accessing the records may need more time and practice to establish the connection, which can take anywhere from a couple of days to even weeks or months before they either get results or feel they've exhausted all possible options for answers.

I read them. Now what?

If you've received your answer, the best thing to do is act on it. The Akashic Records are not meant as entertainment or something to play around with for fun. If you receive an answer that resonates with you and feels authentic, take action immediately so that things can start to change for the better as quickly as possible. If the answer is unclear to you, perhaps you need to further reflect or meditate on it. Sometimes the answer you receive will be a hint designed to lead you towards the real answer. The aim of a hint would be to challenge you enough to help you grow.

Can anyone read my records?

The Akashic Records are not only meant for those permitted by a reader or healer, which is why there's nothing you need to do to give other people access. Anyone can connect with their records and access the information they're looking for.

Accessing anyone else's records needs a lot of training and practice. It is not something that should be attempted by someone new to Akashic Records. If you would like to access your records, please follow the steps listed in this book.

The Akashic Records are a one-of-a-kind way of knowing because the data is all about that individual whose records are accessible, so you must ask for permission to look into their records. You won't learn anything about someone else's soul's journey. You will perceive and learn about their life and what they have chosen to experience in this lifetime, and this is a sacred process that should be used with caution, love, and light.

Is it bad to read my records too often?

No. There is nothing wrong with accessing your Akashic Records if you feel that doing so will provide insight or guidance for improving certain aspects of your life. The only thing we recommend is not getting stuck in the past or constantly revisiting traumatic experiences. The records are meant to provide guidance for the present and future, not keep you stuck in what has already happened.

How do I know that accessing the records worked?

If you feel the information received from the records is accurate and helpful, then it likely worked. However, sometimes people need time for things to start making sense or take effect in their lives. The Akashic Records are not an instant fix that completely changes your life in just one session. Instead, they are meant to provide guidance that will lead you in the right direction.

What kind of knowledge is accessible to you once you've opened the Akashic Records?

You have unlimited access to the Akashic Records. It means you can go back in time and witness your conception, or even forward into the future to see what life may be like for yourself in the years ahead. However, some things will only be visible when you're ready for them based on your spiritual development.

Additionally, the records are a source of information about our lives here on Earth and contain knowledge about other dimensions, parallel universes, and beyond. As you progress on your spiritual path and become more open to expanded consciousness levels, you will gradually access this information, too.

You can get information about business, spirituality, personal growth, relationships, health, and more.

The Akashic Records contain a wealth of knowledge just waiting to be tapped into. So, whatever you're curious about or seek guidance on, the records can likely provide an answer. However, remember that the information received should always be used as a tool to make better choices and not as a way to place blame or judge ourselves or others.

What is an Akashic session? Should you get one?

An Akashic session is when you can access the Akashic Records for guidance and insight on a particular topic or issue in your life.

If you're feeling lost, confused, or stuck, getting an Akashic session with someone trained in accessing and interpreting the records might be helpful. This type of session can help you move forward in life and make better choices for yourself, which is why it's considered a valuable resource.

However, there are also risks involved with accessing the Akashic Records (just like with anything else that deals with the unseen). Some people may not receive accurate information or intuitive guidance, and others may become obsessed with the records and constantly revisiting past events. So, if you do decide to get a session, be sure to take everything with a grain of salt and use your intuition to discern what is right for you.

Can I access the Akashic Records without a session?

Yes, it is possible to access the Akashic Records without a session with someone else. Many people choose to do this on their own to get guidance and insight about specific areas of their lives.

The best way to access the records is through meditation, as this will help you connect with your higher self and allow for greater clarity when seeking information from the Akashic Records.

However, keep in mind that if you choose to do this without a session, it's possible the information obtained will not be 100% accurate or helpful. When we meditate and go inside ourselves, there are infinite possibilities of where our consciousness can travel. But, when another person goes into the records, they have more control over what is seen and felt.

How can you use the Akashic Records in your daily life?

Once you've accessed the records, there are several ways they can improve your daily life:

- They provide guidance for decision-making and solving problems

- Through meditation, you can also receive messages from higher beings and spirit guides offering guidance and support

- They help you connect with your intuition and inner wisdom

- The records can also access other dimensions, parallel universes, and beyond

So, the next time you're feeling lost or stuck, try using the Akashic Records as a tool for guidance and insight. You may be surprised at the amount of information available and how it can help improve your life.

What should I expect from an Akashic session?

When you have an Akashic session, it's essential to remember that the information received should always be used as a tool to help you make better choices and not as a way to place blame or judgment on yourself or others.

Some of the things you may expect from an Akashic session include:

- Guidance on a particular issue or topic
- Insight into your life path and purpose
- Messages from spirit guides or higher beings
- Assistance in decision-making
- Healing past wounds

The Akashic Records are a powerful tool that offers guidance and insight into our lives. So, if you're feeling lost, confused, or stuck, an Akashic session may be the right solution for you.

How does blocked energy affect the Akashic Records?

If there is blocked energy in a particular area of your life, it can also affect your access to the Akashic Records. When we have blockages or stagnant energy in our lives, it creates an obstacle that prevents us from moving forward.

It's important to do some healing work, such as yoga, meditation, or Reiki, to clear away this blocked energy. These methods will help release the stagnant energy and allow greater clarity and insight when accessing the Akashic Records.

So, if you're feeling stuck or blocked in any way, try healing work to clear away the energy. It will help you gain better clarity and access the Akashic Records more easily.

What is Akashic healing?

Akashic healing is a process that helps clear away blocked energy and restore balance in the body. It can be a standalone treatment or in conjunction with other forms of healing, such as Reiki or massage.

The purpose of Akashic healing is to help you release any negative emotions or thoughts that may be blocking your energy. By doing so, you experience greater flow and a sense of harmony with yourself and the world around you.

Through Akashic healing, it's possible to release emotions, such as fear, guilt, shame, or anger that may be blocking your energy channels. Some people also choose to use an Akashic session in conjunction with their treatment, as this helps provide them with a greater sense of insight and connection.

So, if you're feeling blocked or stagnant in any way, try an Akashic session together with healing work like Reiki or massage. You may discover that your energy is restored and flowing more freely than before.

What if I don't believe in past lives?

That's perfectly okay. You don't need to believe in past lives to access the Akashic Records. The records are a repository of information that exists outside of time and space, so our beliefs or our own understanding does not limit them.

So, if you're curious about the records but don't necessarily believe in past lives, you can still access the information available to you.

What is "shadow" work?

Shadow work is the process of exploring and healing the darker aspects of our psyche, including anger, fear, guilt, or shame.

The purpose of shadow work is to bring these darker aspects into the light so that they can be healed and integrated into our lives. By doing this, we create greater balance within ourselves and allow more positive energy to flow through our lives.

So, if you're looking for a way to heal the darker aspects of your psyche, try an Akashic session together with shadow work like yoga or meditation. It will help you clear away any blockages, and your life can be filled with greater peace and joy.

What is karmic debt?

Karmic debt is any unresolved issue or trauma we have carried with us from past lives, including heartache, illness, poverty, and addiction, among others.

Many people feel weighed down by this karmic debt that prevents them from moving forward in their lives. These issues may also manifest as physical symptoms, such as pain or illness.

Working with Akashic Records, you can release this karmic debt and allow a greater sense of peace in your life. It will help you move forward on your journey without being weighed down by past issues that no longer serve you.

What if you don't act on information received in an Akashic Record?

It's okay. You don't have to act on anything you receive during an Akashic session. The records are a tool for self-discovery, so it's up to you whether or not you choose to take any action in response to the information.

For many people, accessing the Akashic Records can be highly empowering as it allows them to take control of their lives.

However, it's important to remember that you are always in charge, and the records will never tell you what to do.

If you're curious about the Akashic Records but unsure if you want to take any action based on the information received, simply observe, and see how you feel. You may find that the information starts resonating with you over time and, eventually, leads you to take action in your life.

Can accessing Akashic Records lead to mental healing?

Some people believe that accessing the Akashic Records leads to mental healing. Many people find that going through their Akashic Records helps them identify and heal the root causes of their mental health issues. If you are struggling with a mental health issue, it might be worth considering whether accessing your Akashic Records could help you heal.

Can Akashic Records reveal past lives?

Yes, the Akashic Records often reveal past lives. Many people find that understanding their past lives is helpful to understand their current life situation.

Will Akashic Records always give me an answer?

No, the Akashic Records will not always give you an answer. Sometimes the records provide more questions than answers because they are a tool for self-discovery, and it's up to you to interpret the information you receive.

However, the records are always accurate and never give you false information. It's up to you to decide what to do with the information you receive.

Can I use Akashic Records for business purposes?

Yes, the Akashic Records can be used for business purposes. Many people find that accessing the records helps them identify and resolve issues affecting their business.

If you're looking for a way to improve your business, consider working with Akashic Records. The records can provide you with valuable insight into what is blocking your success and how you can overcome these obstacles.

When can I expect results from working with Akashic Records?

This is a difficult question to answer as everyone's experience is different. Some people receive results almost immediately after working with Akashic Records. Others take longer to see any changes in their lives.

It's imperative to remember that the records are a tool for self-discovery and will never tell you what to do or give you a solution.

How long is an Akashic Records session?

An Akashic Records session can take anywhere from 45 minutes to an hour, depending on whether there are records that need to be read and how long the person receiving the reading requires to obtain the information.

What should I do after an Akashic Records session?

After receiving your reading, it's important that you reflect upon all of the information you received during your session to integrate it into your life. It's advisable to write down some notes about what resonated with you or spend time meditating on the information you received.

What should I avoid during an Akashic Record reading?

There are a few things to keep in mind when exploring Akashic Records. First, try not to jump ahead of yourself or make assumptions about what you might find during your reading.

It's essential to be open and receptive to the information presented during your session.

Second, avoid coming into an Akashic Record reading with any expectations. Remember, this is a process of self-discovery, and you may not receive all the answers you're looking for. Be patient and allow yourself to explore at your pace.

Third, avoid coming into reading with negativity or judgment. Remember, the Akashic Records are a reflection of your energy, and you will get out of it what you put in. If you approach your session with an open mind and willingness to learn, you will likely find that you receive immense benefit from your reading.

When should you schedule an Akashic Records reading?

There are many different reasons people choose to schedule an Akashic Records reading with a psychic medium. Many people find it helpful when they want to connect with their loved ones who have passed on, and others feel drawn toward exploring the records for personal or spiritual growth purposes.

How often should you access your Akashic Records?

There is no right or wrong answer for how often you should access your Akashic Records. Some people find that they only need to access them once a year, while others regularly explore the records. It's up to you and what feels comfortable for you.

Are Akashic Records open to everyone?

Yes, the Akashic Records are open to everyone. Some people may experience barriers when accessing their records (like spiritual interference), but the ability of individuals is not affected by education level or any other factors, such as nationality or culture.

The Akashic Records are a powerful tool for self-discovery and growth. If you're curious about exploring the records, be sure to keep an open mind and approach your reading with a willingness to learn. The more open you are, the more benefits you will likely receive from your reading.

Chapter 16: Reaching the Akashic Records in 30 Days

As you know by now, the Akashic Records allow us to see the world from an entirely different point of view. The experience helps us grasp a more profound and broader sense of the universe and existence. If you reflect on the daily human experience, you find that most of us get consumed by the mundane dramas, traumas, and issues we face. We often allow ourselves to be weighed down by the heavy energies of the terrestrial plane. However, accessing the Akashic Records takes us to a completely different place, where you can feel your energy being raised. Acquiring the Akashic Records is equivocal to reaching a significantly elevated vibrational plane. At that point, it will feel like all of Earth's dramas, traumas, and issues have been diminished.

When you've accessed the Akashic Records, you've accessed the opportunity to gain clarity of how all your traumas and issues connect. You better understand why you've chosen these challenges, in particular, to work with and overcome during your lifetime. It grants you better awareness of all your opportunities for growth and development and the endless possibilities your decisions have to offer you. This mindset replaces a very low perspective of life, overflowing with problems and obstacles. This experience can be quite opening and may bring your attention to new realizations. You may even come to realize a certain issue or feud is a fragment of a karmic cycle you're destined to bring to an end. Perhaps the most interesting thing about reaching your Akashic Records is learning about all your connections and interactions dating back to and beyond our current space and time and into an entirely alternate timeline and lifetime. These revelations bring your attention to similar issues you've experienced at a specific point in time, and you are here, now, to resolve by acting more wisely and mindfully.

Think of the records as a plane that mirrors everything celestial, reflecting everything we want and all the choices we make. You will likely come in contact with your higher self upon accessing the records, providing you with information about how your choices affected you. It helps you identify whether some of the current aspects of your life aren't aligned with your soul path and, therefore, make you feel drained and unhappy. When you gather clearer insight into the reasoning behind these decisions, you gain the opportunity to rethink your choices and fall in tune with your soul's purpose.

According to metaphysics and psychology, trauma can be inherited via generations. Unlocking your records helps you free yourself of generational karmic debt and pave the way to endless blessings. They are an excellent way to discover your strengths and the weak points that persist in your soul's makeup. Disregarding emotional and mental inadequacies will sooner or later cause them to reveal themselves through physical ailments. Fortunately, the understanding you gather of your innate self helps you come to terms with and even stand up to your traumas, fears, energetic blocks, and unhealthy patterns you've accumulated over a series of lifetimes. You get to identify the things and individuals that no longer serve you and why you continue to attract them into your life. At this point, you have the power to initiate change.

This chapter provides a 30-day guide to reaching your Akashic Records. This guide will help raise your energy and prepare you for the experience. You will also find several best practices and things you shouldn't do when attempting to access the records. Lastly, this chapter includes valuable tips and guidelines.

30-Day Guide to Reaching Akashic Records

You need to ready and prepare yourself before you access your Akashic Records. As explained above, reaching the Akashic Records can and will be a life-changing experience. While it is highly rewarding, it will change your perception of many life aspects and the human experience. Following a 30-day guide that raises your vibrational energy and gains different yet more elevated viewpoints of life will help you embrace the journey with open arms. It also makes it much easier to access the records because, as you may recall, it can take weeks or months to reach them. Preparing yourself for this experience allows you to enter and leave it safely. The following 30-day guide helps you ease in but makes you feel incredibly powerful, balanced, and generally happier.

Day 1

- Drink a glass of water.
- Use incense and sage to cleanse your room.
- Practice mindfulness for 5 minutes.
- Take a 15-minute walk in nature.

Day 2

- Let natural air and light flow into your room.
- Practice visualization for 2 minutes.
- You can visualize anything you desire.

- Ground yourself for 5 minutes.

Day 3

- Say 5 positive affirmations.
- They could be about gratitude, self-love, success, etc.
- Drink a glass of water.
- Do something nice for someone.
- It doesn't have to be a large gesture.
- It can be as little as offering them a bar of chocolate.

Day 4

- Drink a glass of water.
- Eat healthy greens.
- Go for a 30-minute walk.
- Practice mindfulness for 5 minutes.

Day 5

- Practice visualization for 2 minutes.
- You can visualize anything you desire.
- Journal your insights.
- What did you visualize? How did it make you feel? Include details.
- Pet, an animal.

Day 6

- Drink a glass of water.
- Breathe deeply for 2 minutes.
- Think about 3 good things in your life.
- Write them down.

Day 7
- Think about 5 positive qualities in yourself.
- Avoid negative self-talk, even if it were in the context of a joke.
- Don't talk negatively about others.
- Smile at a stranger.

Day 8
- Meditate for 5 minutes.
- Listen to soothing music.
- Don't partake in negative conversations.

Day 9
- Drink a glass of water.
- Go for a long walk through nature.
- Journal your emotions.

Day 10
- Ground yourself for 3 minutes.
- Listen to 144 Hz (third-eye frequency).
- Cleanse your room using incense and sage.

Day 11
- Practice yoga for 15 minutes.
- Take a warm salt bath.
- Go on a social media and technology break.

Day 12
- Drink a glass of water.
- Eat clean foods.
- Have balanced meals.

- Avoid junk food.
- Eat a lot of greens.
- Practice eating only until you're satiated.

Day 13

- Say positive affirmations about yourself.
- Express your gratitude toward others.
- Journal your thoughts and feelings.

Day 14

- Practice mindfulness for 7 minutes.
- Drink a glass of water.
- Go for a 30-minute walk through nature.

Day 15

- Help someone in need.
- Try something new.
- Go for something you never thought you'd do (skydiving, bungee jumping, skiing, horse riding, etc.)
- Write down your experience and how it felt in full detail.

Day 16

- Drink a glass of water.
- Take the stairs instead of the elevator.
- Exercise for 15 minutes.

Day 17

- Avoid toxic people.
- Don't drink alcohol.

- Avoid alcohol for the day and eliminate or reduce it for the remaining 13 days.
- Avoid arguments.

Day 18

- Ground yourself for 5 minutes.
- Take deep breaths for 2 minutes.
- Read a positive article or blog post.

Day 19

- Drink a glass of water.
- Go for a 15-minute walk through nature.
- Allow yourself to wonder about the world.
- Write your questions down.

Day 20

- Drink a glass of water.
- Listen to 144 Hz (third-eye frequency).
- Think about things you wish to learn about yourself and write them down.

Day 21

- Wear your favorite crystal as a necklace or a bracelet.
- Use aromatherapy.
- Journal your thoughts.

Day 22

- Drink a glass of water.
- Listen to 963 Hz (crown chakra frequency).
- Try to connect with your spirit guides.

Day 23
- Go for a 15-minute walk through nature.
- Look out for signs from the universe.
- They could be anything you resonate with (a white butterfly, angel numbers, or recurring words)

Day 24
- Use sage.
- Try out a past life regression meditation.
- Journal your experience.

Day 25
- Drink water.
- Listen to 192 Hz (throat chakra frequency).
- Notice where you felt it and how it made you feel.

Day 26
- Visit a reiki practitioner, get a massage, or indulge in any similar form of energy healing.
- Journal your experience.
- Read Akashic prayers.

Day 27
- Cleanse your room with sage.
- Practice mindfulness for 5 minutes.
- Get in touch with your guides.

Day 28
- Come up with questions surrounding a particular theme in your life.
- Visualize the answers.

- Journal what you saw.

Day 29

- Drink a glass of water.
- Take a long walk through nature.
- Treat yourself to something nice.

Day 30

- Meditate for 5 minutes.
- Read Akashic prayers.
- Journal about the past 30 days.
- Include any remarkable memories, how they felt, and whether you changed in any way (it could be your mindset or the way you feel).

Dos and Don'ts

Now that you've completed the 30-day guide and are ready to access your Akashic Records, it helps to learn about a few best practices and things you can do to help you reach the records more easily. You will also learn what you should avoid prior to and upon your attempt to reach the records.

Dos

- It is recommended that you use your favorite crystals when accessing your Akashic Records. Besides promoting healing, balancing your chakras, and elevating your energies, which are all things you can significantly benefit from when reaching your records, they offer protection. Wearing crystals like hematite, black tourmaline, onyx, or black obsidian as a bracelet or necklace ensures your safety.
- You've probably noticed that drinking a glass of water was a reoccurring task on the 30-day guide. Staying hydrated

is vital for our health, and water is also an excellent conductor of energy. Water fountains are commonly used in feng shui as it aids the movement of energies and the promotion of prosperity. It is highly associated with the flow of good qi (energy). Water flushes out harmful toxins, negatively affecting our vibrational energies. It also facilitates the process of getting in touch with the higher plane.

- Burning sage cleanses and purifies the area, eliminating your body, the surrounding objects, and the overall space of bad energy. This allows you to invite better and more positive energy into your space. It helps you attain a healing state, refine intuition, and connect with the spiritual realm. You should call on your spirit guides to help you purify your space's energy. Ask them, or your archangel, to put a violet flame at the center of your space, at each corner, the window, and on top of each door to ward off beings with lower energies.

- Another reoccurring task in the 30-day guide was grounding yourself and practicing mindfulness techniques. Taking a moment to move around, stretch your body, and ground yourself helps you relax and eliminate any intrusive thoughts or feelings. It helps you stay highly conscious and mindful as you access your records. You also need to keep your eyes wide open as you reach the records. The process is new and possibly sleep-inducing, and you don't want to get drowsy and doze off during your reading.

Don'ts

- While this one may seem like an odd "don't do," it does make a lot of sense. You shouldn't overeat before you attempt to access your Akashic Records. An overly full stomach can make you feel very uncomfortable and tired. It can be incredibly hard to focus after having a heavy meal, making it hard to raise your vibrations and causing you to feel very sleepy and drowsy.

- You shouldn't drink alcohol at least 24 hours prior to your record reading session. Alcohol, as you're probably aware, hinders your balance and composure. It can make you fall out of tune with your mental, physical, and spiritual state, making it nearly impossible to match the vibrational frequency of the higher plane.

- Avoid intense conversations or partaking in quarrels or arguments with others before your record reading session. Arguments significantly lower your vibration. They can diminish your energy and make you feel drained or frustrated. These negative emotions may become too powerful that you cannot focus on anything else.

- You need to avoid noisy environments when you're preparing to access your Akashic Records. Any unwanted elements or distractions can interfere with your vibrational energy. They will also make accessing the higher plane more challenging. Steer clear of loud music, kids, TV, and any other form of noise.

- You should never try to access the Akashic Records when you feel tired. Navigating the higher realm requires a lot of strength, energy, and focus. You don't want to risk feeling even more fatigued. Also, avoid any attempts whenever you're feeling under the weather, stressed, burned out, restless, depressed, or upset. Accessing the records when you feel any form of negativity can be harmful.

Tips and Guidelines

There are some guidelines you need to follow when accessing the Akashic Records. They're not meant to be excessively strict, nor are they aimed at taking the fun out of the process. The main purpose behind these guidelines is to aid you in learning, developing, and growing with the help of the records without hindering or affecting your experience in any way.

- **Stay Present and Conscious**

It's crucial to be present in your body and conscious of your being. The 30-day guide included various tasks related to mindfulness and grounding for this reason. The more you practice, the easier it is to implement them in your record accessing experience. As mentioned above, you also need to keep your eyes open during practice. It is something most clairvoyants struggle with. If you are a clairvoyant, you may struggle to visualize with your eyes open. If this is the case, rehearse, closing your eyes for one or two minutes to visualize an image and gather some insight before you open your eyes once again. You may find it easier to fixate your eyes on a blank wall, so it's easier to "see" pictures and things through your mind's eye. It helps to practice the visualization tasks in the 30-day guide with open eyes. In time, you will see vivid images with your eyes open.

- **Make It a Habit**

Once you get the hang of it, make sure to access your records frequently, as they can serve as an indispensable guide in your daily life. Integrating it as a habit can change your personal and professional life. You might even want to access your records multiple times throughout the day since you can receive, feel, hear, know, and intuitively get in touch with information as needed. Therefore, you benefit immensely from learning to access your records with your eyes wide open.

- **Use Your Full Legal Name**

You shouldn't necessarily use your maiden or birth name to access your records. Instead, make sure to use the name found in your legal records, like your passport or driver's license. If you don't use your legal name, you might realize your record lacks the full information. Using a nickname or even your spiritual name only grants you access to a small part of your Akashic Records.

- **Read Your Prayers - Don't Memorize Them**

Words carry vibrations. They are symbols that donate energy levels upon being read, seen, or heard. Reading a prayer aloud can hold so much power since you are reading, hearing, and feeling it and its energy simultaneously.

With repetition, you'll find that the prayers have embedded themselves in your brain. Even then, try not to mindlessly recite them. This is one aspect where your ability to channel your intention will serve you greatly.

- **Actively and Deliberately Seek Answers**

Deliberately seek answers for your questions, as this will deepen your acknowledgment and recognition of the information you receive. Accessing the Akashic Records is a process that highly depends on asking questions you want to explore. It helps to write down at least 5 to 7 questions surrounding a single theme you wish to understand more deeply. Asking questions about different unrelated topics will not be a great help. Meanwhile, receiving various pieces of information regarding one issue allows you to put the fragments together to complete one large picture.

- **Be Ethical and Righteous**

When you're working with the Akashic Records, make sure to ask questions about you and only you. You can learn endless things about yourself, so you need to make the best use of this time and discover the different facets of your being. It is your opportunity to focus on and uncover who you are and identify the things holding you back from aligning with your soul's purpose and achieving your goals. It is your chance to ask about why you've chosen your family and life or what your next huge step is. You shouldn't be interfering in other people's affairs, even if they're slightly related to you. For instance, while it is tempting, you shouldn't ask if your significant other is cheating on you. This is a question that goes beyond your integrity. A better question would be, "what is blocking me from feeling close to my partner?" Use this time to receive answers that will help you grow as a person. You need the information to boost your spiritual growth and walk your soul path.

- **Keep Your Akashic Prayers on You**

Whether it's a picture of the prayers or a note that you carry around in your wallet, you should always keep your Akashic prayers on you. Not just so you can access the realm whenever needed, but so you can also familiarize yourself with the prayers. The same way a musician benefits from listening to music and an actor benefits from listening to monologues, you, too, would benefit from having the prayers become a part of your daily life.

- **Don't Teach the Prayers**

Becoming a practitioner with enough expertise to teach others takes a lot of time, dedication, and effort. Teaching others to access the Akashic realm is a huge responsibility. While the practice may seem simple enough, the prayers are incredibly powerful. If treated with disrespect and carelessness, a great deal of karma could be inflicted on the doer. This isn't something that should be taught quickly out of excitement. If you want to benefit a friend, refer them to a professional resource instead.

- **Consistency Is Key**

Consider accessing your Akashic Records once every day for a month. Make sure to journal your insights each time. You can start with 25 minutes of writing and work your way up whenever you can. Training to access your records and delving deeper into your insights come with practice. Many people struggle with physical fatigue at first since they aren't used to the high vibrational frequencies of energy. However, you should not find it too hard as the 30-day guide is designed to ease you into the process and raise your overall energy. You may feel tired at first, considering that the Akashic Records are on a much higher energy level.

- **Be Patient**

We've mentioned above that the road towards fluently accessing the Akashic realm is long and winding. In the same way it requires discipline and consistency, it also requires a lot of patience. On the days when you are feeling emotionally and spiritually drained, do not punish yourself. Rest days have been included in the 30-day guide, but we must reiterate the importance of allowing yourself to rest without any guilt. This is especially true if you're the type of person who would work out seven days a week because they'd rather not waste time.

- **Be Gentle**

On the days when you feel like you haven't progressed, do not put yourself down. Accept that you won't always be met with progress, but that does not mean your efforts were wasted. Keep your eyes on the fact that you are on your own team; you are not the enemy.

Accessing the Akashic Records allows you to see life from a complete viewpoint. It helps you remember and regain touch with who you genuinely are in essence and in-depth. Ultimately, you remember that you are a divine, infinite soul and your human experience is a game, at least for the time being. The entire process of getting to and experiencing the Akashic Records aims to raise your vibrational frequency. You can't access the records until you're ready, and to be ready, you must implement several changes into your lifestyle and habits. These changes are all positive, which will undoubtedly improve your overall quality of life, meaning that the process, from start to finish, is transformative and highly rewarding.

Conclusion

Now that you have all of this knowledge, it's time to put it into practice. You can make a habit of daily meditation and journaling about the experiences you had through your journeys. These are a few benefits you will receive from regularly connecting with your spirit guides.

We hope that if you were confused about the Akashic Records before, you now have a better understanding of what they are and how to connect with them.

The main thing we want everyone who reads this book to take away our knowledge and inspiration. We encourage you to continue learning about the Akashic Records and use them as a tool for personal growth. As you raise your vibration and connect with your spirit guides, you will access more information from the records. This knowledge will help you live a happier and more fulfilling life.

We studied various techniques in this book and encouraged you to try them all. Find the ones that work best for you and stick with them. The more you practice, the easier it becomes to connect with your spirit guides and access the Akashic Records.

Karma is a powerful force that manifests into our lives through the Akashic Records. It helps to understand what karma is, how it works, and how it can be changed. We hope this book has provided you with knowledge on how to do just that.

Now you also know more about your chakras and how to unblock them. There are many ways to do this, and we covered some of them in this book. Again, find the ones that work best for you, and keep practicing until they become second nature.

Reading the records can be very overwhelming at first, but over time it becomes easier. There is a lot of information in the Akashic Records, so don't feel like you have to take it all in one sitting. This can also be said for anything else that is challenging in life. Don't let it stop you from moving forward. Practice multiple techniques until you find the ones that work best for you, and keep learning as much as you can. With time and dedication, you will connect with your spirit guides and easily access the Akashic Records.

While the information in this book may seem overwhelming at first, don't let it intimidate you. You don't have to read the book cover-to-cover in one sitting, nor do you have to practice all of the steps daily. We recommend you take your time and return to it when you need help with something specific.

We want to leave you with one final thought. The Akashic Records are an infinite source of knowledge and wisdom. As you continue to connect with them, you will access more and more of this information. We sincerely hope you use this power for the good of all beings.

Here's another book by Silvia Hill that you might like

Free limited time bonus

Stop for a moment. I have a free bonus set up for you. The problem is that we forget 90% of everything that we read after 7 days. Crazy fact, right? Here's the solution: we've created a printable, 1-page pdf summary for this book that you're reading now. All you have to do to get your free pdf summary is to go to the following website: **https://livetolearn.lpages.co/silviahill/**
Once you do, it will be intuitive. Enjoy, and thank you!

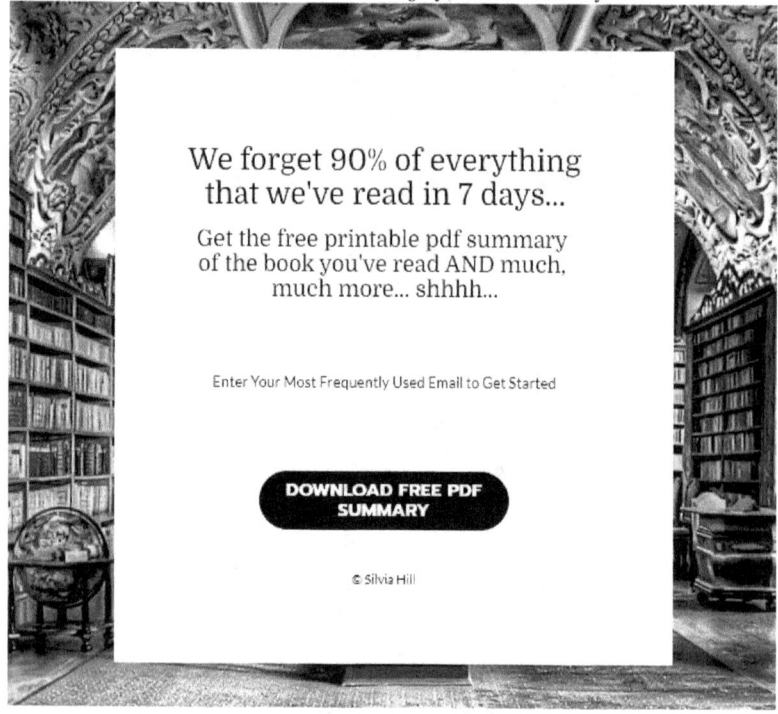

References

Akasa. (n.d.). Theosophy.World. Retrieved from https://www.theosophy.world/encyclopedia/akasa

Akasha and the Akashic Records. (2014, March 27). Blavatskytheosophy.Com. https://blavatskytheosophy.com/Akasha-and-the-Akashic-records

Nash, A. (2020). The Akashic Records: Origins and relation to western concepts. Central European Journal for Contemporary Religion, 3(2), 109–124.

Planes in Theosophy. (n.d.). Theosophy.World. Retrieved from https://www.theosophy.world/encyclopedia/planes-theosophy

What are the Five Elements or Pancha Bhutas? (2021, May 21). Sadhguru.Org. https://isha.sadhguru.org/us/en/wisdom/article/five-elements-pancha-bhuta

Holisticism. (2019, June 28). What Are The Akashic Records? Retrieved from Holisticism website: https://medium.com/holisticism/what-are-the-Akashic-records-ede3bee05673

Neil. (2019, October 29). Akashic Records Benefits - Check out the benefits that you can access. Retrieved from GlobalAkasha.com website: https://globalAkasha.com/Akashic-records-benefits

Wigington, P. (n.d.). Understanding the Akashic Records and how to access them. Retrieved from Learnreligions.com website: https://www.learnreligions.com/Akashic-records-4783264

Hardman, J. (2020, September 11). Here's how the Akashic Records can help heal your deepest wounds. Thoughtcatalog.Com. https://thoughtcatalog.com/josephine-hardman/2020/09/heres-how-the-Akashic-records-can-help-heal-your-deepest-wounds

Jayaram, V. (n.d.). The concept of karma in Hinduism. Hinduwebsite.Com. Retrieved from https://www.hinduwebsite.com/conceptofkarma.asp

Regan, S. (2020, July 17). 4 signs you're receiving A karmic lesson & how to take action. Mindbodygreen.Com; mindbodygreen. https://www.mindbodygreen.com/articles/signs-youre-receiving-a-karmic-lesson-and-what-to-do-about-it

What A karmic cycle is and 8 things you can do to break it. (2020, September 18). Herway.Net. https://herway.net/what-a-karmic-cycle-is

What is a karmic cycle, and how to break a karmic cycle. (2020, March 29). Themindfool.Com. https://themindfool.com/karmic-cycle

Ferrante, C. (2021, March 23). I'm an Akashic Records reader, and here's what to expect during a reading with me. Retrieved from Well+Good website: https://www.wellandgood.com/what-are-Akashic-records

Holisticism. (2019, June 28). What Are The Akashic Records? Retrieved from Holisticism website: https://medium.com/holisticism/what-are-the-Akashic-records-ede3bee05673

Jonathan, O. (2020, November 18). How to unblock each chakra. Retrieved from Laquilaactive.com website: https://laquilaactive.com/how-to-unblock-each-chakra

Lindberg, S. (2020, August 24). What are chakras? Meaning, location, and how to unblock them. Retrieved from Healthline.com website: https://www.healthline.com/health/what-are-chakras

Stelter, G. (2016, October 4). Chakras: A beginner's guide to the 7 chakras. Retrieved from Healthline.com website: https://www.healthline.com/health/fitness-exercise/7-chakras

5 ways to open your heart chakra - goodnet. (n.d.). Retrieved from Goodnet.org website: https://www.goodnet.org/articles/5-ways-to-open-your-heart-chakra

Bertone, H. J., CNHP, PMP, & Hoshaw, C. (2021, October 20). 9 types of meditation: Which one is right for you? Healthline.Com. https://www.healthline.com/health/mental-health/types-of-meditation

Psycom.Net - mental health treatment resource since 1996. (n.d.). Psycom.Net. Retrieved from https://www.psycom.net/anxiety-test

Reiki Self-Treatment. (n.d.). Clevelandclinic.Org. Retrieved from https://my.clevelandclinic.org/health/treatments/21080-reiki-self-treatment

Villines, Z. (2021, April 21). Anxiety and brain fog: Symptoms, causes, and treatment.

Medicalnewstoday.Com. https://www.medicalnewstoday.com/articles/anxiety-and-brain-fog

Blanchard, T. (2021, August 26). How to use incense for cleansing and protection?

Outofstress.Com; Outofstress.com.

https://www.outofstress.com/incense-for-cleansing-protection

Cho, A. (n.d.). How to smudge your house to invite positive energy. Thespruce.Com. Retrieved from https://www.thespruce.com/how-to-smudge-your-house-1274692

Page, K., & Jane, P. (2017, December 9). 30 sacred herbs for smudging and cleansing purposes. Ilmypsychicjane.Com. https://www.ilmypsychicjane.com/single-post/2017/12/09/30-sacred-herbs-for-smudging-and-cleansing-purposes

Use the power of sound to clear + cleanse your space. (n.d.). Energymuse.Com. Retrieved from https://www.energymuse.com/blog/power-of-sound-clearing

Beckler, M. (2020, June 7). How to connect with your Spirit Guides in 5 steps... Ask for help! Ask-Angels.Com. https://www.ask-angels.com/spiritual-guidance/connect-spirit-guides

DestinationDeluxe. (2020, December 30). Akashic Records – What are they? How do I read the Akashic Records? Destinationdeluxe.Com. https://destinationdeluxe.com/2020/12/30/Akashic-records-reading

Five steps to deepen your relationship with your spirit guide. (n.d.). Kripalu.Org. Retrieved from https://kripalu.org/resources/five-steps-deepen-your-relationship-your-spirit-guide

Hess, A. (n.d.). Soul Realignment. Retrieved from Soulrealignment.com website: http://www.soulrealignment.com/the-Akashic-records-intuition-and-commitment

Higson, A. (2019, March 25). How an Akashic Records Prayer works with intention. Retrieved from Realitymanifestation.com website: https://www.realitymanifestation.com/Akashic-records-prayer

Marlene, C. (2018, October 3). Setting intention as spiritual practice. Retrieved from

Cherylmarlene.com website:

https://www.cherylmarlene.com/setting-intention-as-spiritual-practice

Ysette. (2017, August 8). What is a quality Akashic Record reading? 2/6: INTENTION. Retrieved from Mindsonfire.org website: http://mindsonfire.org/2017/08/08/what-is-a-quality-Akashic-record-reading-pt-26-intention

How to access your own Akashic Records. (n.d.). Retrieved from Healyourlife.com website: https://www.healyourlife.com/how-to-access-your-own-Akashic-records

Neil. (2019, November 10). The Sacred Prayer, Pathway Prayer, and variations. -. Retrieved from GlobalAkasha.com website: https://globalAkasha.com/the-sacred-prayer-pathway-prayer-and-variations

thejoywithin. (2019, April 14). Accessing your Akashic Records through prayer and meditation. Retrieved from Thejoywithin.org website: https://thejoywithin.org/spirituality/accessing-your-Akashic-records-through-prayer-and-meditation

A 6-minute breathing meditation to cultivate mindfulness - mindful. (2016, February 26). Mindful.Org. https://www.mindful.org/a-five-minute-breathing-meditation

Beckler, M. (2019, December 14). How to Access the Akashic Records. Ask-Angels.Com.

https://www.ask-angels.com/spiritual-guidance/access-Akashic-records

Kate. (2021, August 14). What are the Akashic Records, and how to access them.

Katestrong.Com. https://www.katestrong.com/what-are-the-Akashic-records-and-how-to-access-them

Mindfulness: How to do it. (2019, October 18). Mindful.Org.

https://www.mindful.org/mindfulness-how-to-do-it

Victoria, Wille, Crystal, & Jas. (2020, July 17). Akashic Records 101: How to Access and Read your Records.

Alittlesparkofjoy.Com. https://www.alittlesparkofjoy.com/Akashic-records

Insight Network, Inc. (n.d.). No title. Insighttimer.Com. Retrieved from https://insighttimer.com/tomevans/guided-meditations/a-journey-to-the-akaskic

Lauren. (2015, July 31). How to Access the Mysteries of your Akashic Records. Fractalenlightenment.Com. https://fractalenlightenment.com/35113/life/how-to-access-the-mysteries-of-your-Akashic-records

Neil. (2019, October 20). How to access your Own Akashic Records - Global Akasha. GlobalAkasha.Com. https://globalAkasha.com/how-to-access-your-own-Akashic-records

Neuroscience News. (2020, May 6). How strong is your mental imagery? It might depend on how "excitable" your neurons are - Neuroscience News. Neurosciencenews.Com. https://neurosciencenews.com/mental-imagery-neurons-16345

Akashic Records FAQ. (2018, December 19). Retrieved from Mariekecahill.com website: https://mariekecahill.com/about/Akashic-faq

HOW TO READ THE AKASHIC RECORDS OF OTHERS - And what to watch out for when looking for a reader. (2021, March 21). Retrieved from https://www.youtube.com/watch?v=npFUg4dJyp4

Accessing the Akashic Records - FAQs -. (2015, November 23). Akashicfocus.Com. https://Akashicfocus.com/about-Akashic-records/faq-2

Akashic Records FAQ. (2020, April 9). Nancykern.Com.

https://www.nancykern.com/Akashic-records-faq

Marlene, C. (2021, July 3). Akashic Records FAQ. Cherylmarlene.Com.

https://www.cherylmarlene.com/Akashic-records-faq

8 ways to raise your vibration (your positive energy). (n.d.). Retrieved from

Theholisticingredient.com website:

https://www.theholisticingredient.com/blogs/wholesome-living/13587702-8-ways-to-raise-your-vibration-your-positive-energy

Barnett, L. (2015). The Infinite Wisdom of the Akashic Records: How to access your soul's plan with ease. Red Wheel/Weiser.

O'Connor, B. (2015, June 4). 11 water practices for healing. Retrieved from

Spiritualityhealth.com website:

https://www.spiritualityhealth.com/blogs/heart-health/2015/06/04/bess-oconnor-16-ways-change-your-vibration-water

satomikeely. (2021, March 8). Accessing the Akashic Records: How to make the process easier - smile love shine. Retrieved from Smileloveshine.com website:

https://smileloveshine.com/accessing-the-Akashic-records-how-to-make-the-process-easier

White, A. (2018, July 18). 11 benefits of burning sage, how to get started, and more. Retrieved from Healthline.com website: https://www.healthline.com/health/benefits-of-burning-sage